CHEVROLET BIG-BLOCK MUSCLE CARS

Anthony Young

Motorbooks International
Publishers & Wholesalers

First published in 1993 by Motorbooks International Publishers & Wholesalers, PO Box 2, 729 Prospect Avenue, Osceola, WI 54020 USA

Motorbooks International books are also available at discounts in bulk quantity for industrial or sales-promotional use. For details write to Special Sales Manager at the Publisher's address

Library of Congress Cataloging-in-Publication Data Available
ISBN 0-87938-725-4

Printed and bound in Hong Kong

On the front cover: The most awesome display of Chevrolet big-block power on the street was the 450hp 454ci LS6, optional only in the Chevelle SS454 in 1970 and 1971. A higher-compression mechanical cam version, the LS7, was available over the Chevy parts counter. *Mike Mueller*

On the frontispiece: The aluminum block 427ci ZL-1 marked the apex of big-block development. In 1969 it was offered as an RPO in the Corvette and as a Central Office Production Order (COPO) in the Camaro. This is the engine compartment of ZL-1 Corvette Serial No. 29219, owned by Roger Judski. *Mike Mueller*

On the title page: The new Mk IV 396ci V-8 in 1967 made the first generation Camaro an awesome street performer and helped establish it as a leader in the pony car class. *Mike Mueller*

On the back cover: The 454ci big-block was dropped from Chevrolet passenger cars in the midseventies, but it has remained available in trucks since 1970. The 454 SS pickup boasting the new Mk V generation V-8 with performance enhancements was introduced in 1991. *Chevrolet.* *Inset:* The Mk V 454ci V-8 features throttle body injection, computer control, and other refinements that enable the big-block to move into the 21st century. *Chevrolet*

Contents

Acknowledgments

The Chevrolet big-block V-8 story really should have been recorded years ago when a number of the principal players were still alive and had clear recollections. Key among these were Edward N. Cole, Harry Barr, Vince Piggins, and Cal Wade. It is a tremendous loss to Chevrolet enthusiasts that no one ever sat down with the ever-dynamic Piggins and got the whole inside story from him on all of his involvement with Chevrolet high-performance engines and cars. And certainly one of the most colorful, charismatic, and influential men at Chevrolet was Zora Arkus-Duntov. Why no automotive journalist snagged Arkus-Duntov the day after he retired and recorded every facet of his rich and rewarding career and contributions at Chevrolet is a profound question.

Fortunately, a number of key engineers are still alive and have astounding memories for detail. Much of this book involves their recollections. I would like to thank Maurice S. ("Rosy") Rosenberger, Don McPherson, Dick Keinath, Gib Huffsteader, E.O. ("Eli") Whitney, Bill Howell, Fred Frincke, Art Casper, Dave Martens, Mark McPhail, Tom Langdon, Scott Leon, and Jim Minneker for recounting their work on the Chevrolet big-block V-8.

Thanks to the contacts I made while writing *Chevrolet Small-Block V-8*, the job of writing this companion book on the Chevrolet big-block V-8 was made much easier.

Mike Mueller, who shot the cover photo of the 1967 Camaro Z-28 for the small-block V-8 book, did the primary color photography for this book. His sense of composition and willingness to go anywhere to photograph big-block Chevys helped to make this book what it is. It is a pleasure to work with such a professional.

I would like to thank photographer Thomas Glatch of Wauwatosa, Wisconsin, for the color shots of the ZR2. I can't imagine doing a book on the Chevrolet big-block V-8 without including the Big Doggie.

My request for many of the black-and-white photos was handled by Mark Broderick in Chevrolet Public Relations. This book would not have been possible without his help.

Kari St. Antoine, in charge of Media Relations in Chevrolet Public Relations, set up interviews with Scott Leon at the Desert Proving Grounds and Jim Minneker, chief of Corvette Powertrain Development, in order for me to get the ZR2 story. She also handled my request to reproduce the "Some Pieces Are Sold Separately" ad shown in the chapter covering the

454ci V-8. Cheryl A. Morgan, account executive with D'Arcy, Masius, Benton & Bowles, obtained permission from General Motors (GM) Service Parts Operations for me to use the ad in this book and sent a proof copy for reproduction.

Two people at GM Powertrain deserve particular thanks for all their efforts on my behalf. Jack Underwood, product information coordinator for V-8 engines, was tireless in his efforts to line up interviews, go through his files for pertinent black-and-white as well as color photos, and get copies of division documents and other papers to help me record the big-block story. Louis Ironside, also in Product Information, brought forth binders full of photo numbers with subject descriptions carefully logged years ago by an unknown hand. He also told me tragic stories of all the papers, photos, and other relevant materials that over the years have been carelessly thrown away by others who had no idea of their historical significance.

Kathy Nagorny, Motor Vehicle Manufacturers' Association (MVMA) coordinator in product information, could not have been more thorough or helpful in supplying me with the Automobile Manufacturers Association and MVMA specifications covering the

348ci, 409ci, 396/402ci, 427ci, and 454ci V-8s. These documents were particularly helpful in accurately giving the specifications of such exotic big-block V-8s as the L88 and ZL-1.

The people at the Tonawanda Engine Plant supplied photos both outside and inside the home of the Chevy big-block V-8.

Rick Vogelin, of High Performance Communications and editor of *Chevy Thunder,* supplied the photos of the 454ci H.O. (High Output) and 502ci short-block engines.

I would like to thank the Beach Boys, Brother Records, and Capitol Industries for permission to reproduce the *Little Deuce Coupe* album cover.

Special thanks go to the owners of the Chevy big-block cars showcased in the book. In the chapter covering the 348, these vehicles include Walter Cutlip's 1958 Impala and Jim Hissel's 1961 Impala.

In the chapter on the 409, Marty Locke's 1961 Impala SS and Rudy and Kathy Sasina's 1965 Impala SS add much to the book.

The chapter on the 396 contains a 1965 Corvette from the Lukason & Son Collection, Jim and Gina Collins' 1967 RS Camaro SS, the 1969 Nova SS396 owned by Dan Bennett and Jim Beckerle, and the 1969 Chevelle SS396 sedan with the rare L89 aluminum cylinder head option owned by Roger Adkins.

For the chapter on the 427, Mike Mueller photographed Don Springer's 1967 Impala SS427 and Jim Price's 1969 ZL-1 Camaro.

I particularly want to thank Roger and David Judski for their willingness and patience while Mike Mueller photographed Roger's magnificent 1969 ZL-1 Corvette and 1967 L88 Corvette.

Rounding out the chapter on the 454 are Tim Smith's 1970 Monte Carlo SS454; a 1970 Caprice Sport Coupe owned by Sullivan Chevrolet of Champaign, Illinois; and the cover car, the 1970 LS6 Chevelle SS454 convertible owned by the Lukason & Son Collection.

Due to space limitations, Sam Pierce's 1962 Zintsmaster Impala Super Stock and Gary and Shelly Place's 1969 Yenko Chevelle could not be included in the book.

Finally, I want to thank my wife, Annie, for her support in seeing this book to completion.

This is for you, Erin and Katie.

In 1968, Chevrolet introduced the restyled Corvette with striking lines strongly influenced by the 1965 Mako Shark II show car. The 427ci big-block V-8 was offered in four versions: the 390hp L36, the 400hp L68, the 435hp L71, and the magnificent 430hp L88 with aluminum cylinder heads. Chevrolet

Introduction

The Chevrolet big-block V-8 story is almost as long and illustrious as that of the small-block V-8. The small-block V-8 was introduced in 1955 with a displacement of 265 cubic inches (ci). As justifiably proud of the small-block V-8 as Edward N. Cole and his team of engineers were, a substantially larger and more powerful engine would allow Chevrolet to compete more aggressively against other manufacturers with V-8s of well over 300ci in cars and trucks. Shortly after the release of the small-block V-8 in 1955, the division began work on an engine it called the W-engine.

In 1958, Chevrolet introduced its first big-block, the 348ci V-8. This new engine was a radical departure from the norms of V-8 engine design, with its curious cylinder head-to-cylinder block configuration. This engineering route was pursued for valid manufacturing reasons. Despite claims made to the contrary, the 348 was not designed strictly as a truck engine; it was developed to be installed in both cars and trucks. The goal was to create an engine that could be used in a broad range of applications while reducing tooling and manufacturing costs compared with those of the small-block V-8. What the powerplant

was *not* designed for was racing, but of course it was raced–and it raced well.

In 1961, Chevrolet introduced the 409ci V-8, a bored and stroked version of the 348. Chevrolet offered high-performance options that gave bow-tie enthusiasts all they could ask for; drag racers were delighted to learn that the 409 had been designed with them in mind; and the bigger big-block continued to make Chevrolets the cars to be reckoned with in National Association for Stock Car Auto Racing (NASCAR) events. This emphasis on performance was subtle in Chevrolet's advertising and brochures, but the enthusiast magazines picked up on it right away. The Beach Boys even immortalized the engine in their Top Ten hit "409."

The 409 added immeasurably to Chevrolet's image as a builder of performance street cars and boosted its potential to win circle track events. Still, the very features that made the W-engine a good passenger car and truck engine made it a less-than-ideal NASCAR powerplant. This was no startling revelation–simply an inescapable reality.

Thus was launched the automotive equivalent of the Manhattan Project. When the resulting engine made its debut at the 1963 Daytona 500, it was appropriately dubbed the Mystery En-

gine. A General Motors (GM) edict halted further development of that racing engine, but it was the basis for the first Mark (Mk) IV big-block V-8–the 396–and a new era in street performance was launched.

The 396 won Chevy enthusiasts over as the 348 and 409 never had. It formed the basis of Chevrolet's first muscle car, the Chevelle SS396. From the start, the Mk IV big-block was a superb engine, capable of making a name for itself on the street and the strip.

The 427ci V-8 followed in 1966. The numbers 4-2-7 were magic on the fenders of a Chevrolet, and an even higher level of performance was attained. This version was installed in the Corvette and full-size Chevrolets, but visionary entrepreneurs like Don Yenko, Joel Rosen, and others stuffed 427s in Camaros and Chevelles. Even Chevrolet got into the act with its secretive Central Office Production Order (COPO) cars like the ZL-1 Camaro. A great deal of development went into the all-aluminum 427 ZL-1, with technological fallout that was seen in Can-Am race cars.

Those who couldn't afford the exotic ZL-1 were offered the iron block and head L72, the aluminum head L88, and the Tri-Power L68 and L71, to name just a few. It was the late sixties–the heyday of performance cars–and Chevrolets were among the most respected vehicles, both on the street and on the track. But the push to ever-more displacement and power didn't end there.

In 1970, Chevrolet introduced the 454. Little did the company know just how long its latest big-block would remain in production. Despite the decline of performance in the early seventies and the move to drop the 454 in passenger cars during the mid-seventies, the 454 remained in production for use by boat racers as well as drag racers and in Chevrolet's line of trucks.

The inherent integrity of design engineering that was established with the 396 has served the Mark Series of engines well. With technological advances made in the nineties, it's clear the Chevrolet big-block V-8 will continue to meet the needs of enthusiasts into the twenty-first century.

The biggest of the big blocks ever offered in full-sized Chevrolet passenger cars was the 454ci engine. Equipped with a 454, this

1970 Caprice was the epitome of power and elegance. Mike Mueller

Chapter 1

The 348

The Least Known Big-Block Breaks Ground

That engine was a fairly decent engine, a rugged
engine, but it had a poor combustion
chamber and didn't breathe well.

–Don McPherson

The Turbo-Thrust 348ci V-8 is probably the least known engine in the big-block family. Few examples still exist, and it does not have the cachet of the 409ci V-8 that followed. The W-engine, as it was called by its engineers, was conceived to broaden the range of engine sizes for Chevrolet's cars and trucks. Prior to its introduction in 1958, Chevrolet had only its 235ci inline six-cylinder engine and the popular 265ci and 283ci V-8s available.

The terms *small-block* and *big-block* were coined after the 348ci V-8 was released, to help differentiate the two engines because the 348 was radically different from the 283. Its bore centers, overall length, width, and height all differed from those of the small-block. Even the cylinder head and valve juxtaposition was unique to the 348. Virtually all of its parts were unique to this new engine.

Chevrolet began studies of a larger-displacement V-8 in 1955. Because of the thin-wall casting of the small-block V-8, Chevrolet engineers did not

The Impala was a new top-of-the-line–model Chevrolet introduced for 1958. It was offered as a two-door sport coupe and a convertible.

believe the 283 could be enlarged sufficiently to meet design goals established for the new engine. Later, this would prove not to be the case, as the small-block was eventually enlarged to 327ci, 350ci, and 400ci. Nevertheless, in 1955, Chevrolet engineers felt that to have a significantly larger V-8 would require the research, design, and development of a new V-8.

Chevrolet felt it needed an engine such as the W-engine for several reasons. Demand for automatic transmissions in the company's deluxe line of cars was rising, so Chevrolet had to consider increasing displacement in order to provide the best low-speed and midrange performance. At the time, Chevrolet was developing the two-speed Turboglide transmission, and it was felt that a larger engine with good torque characteristics would work extremely well with the new transmission. Also, other manufacturers already had V-8 engines with displacements over 300ci. For instance, Chrysler had just introduced its 331ci hemi-head FirePower V-8, which instantly became the talk of the industry. Finally, Chevrolet felt that the same basic engine could be used in trucks it was building at the time to give them a higher gross vehicle weight.

The Chevrolet was new from the ground up in 1958. Desirable options included Level Air suspension and the new 348ci big-block V-8.

After releasing the small-block 265ci V-8 in 1955 and 283ci V-8 in 1957, Chevrolet introduced the big-block 348ci V-8 in 1958. In standard tune, the four-barrel 348 produced 250hp at 4400rpm and 355lb-ft of torque at 2800rpm. The 348 was offered through the 1961 model year.

The 348ci V-8 had a bore of 4.125in and a stroke of 3.25in. Bore spacing was 4.84in. The crankshaft and connecting rods were forged steel, and the pistons were cast aluminum. The 348ci V-8 was manufactured and assembled exclusively at Chevrolet's Tonawanda Engine Plant in Tonawanda, New York, a big-block tradition that endures to this day.

The company built two prototype engines of approximately 300ci having the same basic dimensions as the 265ci small-block. One engine was designated X and the other Y. The X-engine received its larger displacement by having engineers increase the bore to 4 inches (in) while retaining the 4.4in bore spacing of the small-block. This required joining, or *siamesing* the bore jackets.(The same operation was also done later with the 400ci small-block V-8 introduced in 1970.) The X-engine's stroke of 3in. matched that of the small-block. This effectively put the displacement at 302ci. Casting this engine block proved difficult because the foundry did not yet have the expertise to do this kind of casting.

The Y-engine received its increased displacement by having its bore enlarged from 3.75in to 3.81in and its stroke increased from 3in to 3.3in. The resulting displacement was 301ci. Besides requiring completely new tools for the crankshaft, this design limited further increases in displacement and compression ratios.

The X- and Y-prototype engines were efforts to determine what would and would not work for a larger-displacement V-8, based on available technology. Chevrolet engineers determined they could not achieve their goals using the same bore centers of 4.4in that were used with the 265ci and 283ci V-8s. That meant the basic engine block dimensions could not be shared with the small-block, and this new engine would need its own machining line as well as assembly line. It was important to discover these needs early in the project.

Because of increasing customer demand, Chevrolet in 1956 considered increasing the number of lines to machine and assemble its 265ci and forthcoming 283ci V-8s.

In a Society of Automotive Engineers (SAE) paper titled "Engineering the 'W' Engine," presented in March of 1958 before the SAE National Passen-

Next page
The 1958 Chevrolet was a departure from the trim design of the 1955–57 models, but this followed an industry trend. The convertible's lines carried the car's increased overall dimensions well. More than 55,000 Impala convertibles were built in 1958.

The combustion chamber–in–block design was chosen by Al Kolbe and based on a similar design used some years before by Mercedes-Benz. The cylinder block deck surface was not perpendicular to the bore, but tilted 16 degrees toward the intake side.

ger Car, Body and Materials Meeting in Detroit, authors John T. Rausch, Howard H. Kehrl, and Donald H. McPherson explained: "If we were going to add to our investment, the cost would not be greatly increased by providing the added lines with a design which could add materially to the displacement range for passenger cars. The same basic engine could be used for the high GVW [gross vehicle weight] truck models which Chevrolet is now building. As a result of these considerations, Management approved our proposal to develop an entirely new engine."

Design Objectives

Just as the small-block V-8 was conceived as primarily a passenger car engine, the big-block, as it had been dubbed, would be used in both cars and trucks. With that basic criterion in mind, Chevrolet established the primary objectives of this new V-8:

1. Adaptability to a broad range of displacement with a minimum number of different parts.

2. Adaptability to a broad range of compression ratios to match the octane trend of future fuels.

3. Compatibility of dimensions with the anticipated space limitations of passenger car designs.

The W-engine got its moniker from the position of the intake and exhaust valves. No combustion chamber was used in the cylinder head. Instead, the combustion chamber was formed by the cylinder bore and piston at top dead center.

4. Provisions for mounting accessories on engines for both passenger cars and trucks.

5. Flexibility of machine tools to accommodate future engine modifications.

Displacement

"Fulfilling the first requirement, adaptability to a broad range of displacement, was a rather straightforward job," the engineers wrote in their 1958 SAE paper. "After establishing the bore and stroke to provide a displacement in line with passenger car requirements, we determined the bore size that would satisfy our maximum displacement truck engine requirements. The largest bore size then established the bore centers that would provide full circumference cooling and minimum core thickness between bores which would be acceptable to the foundry."

Also of concern to the engineers was the juxtaposition of the intake and exhaust valves. With the future displacement increases anticipated, valve sizes would have to increase too. If intake and exhaust valves were positioned inline, as with the small-block V-8, the overall length of the engine, as well as the bore centers, would have to be increased. In addition, the two inboard exhaust valves would be too close to each other to provide adequate valve cooling. Staggering the valves would allow for future valve size increases, provide adequate cooling, and keep the engine block length to a minimum.

Individual mounting bosses for the rocker arms were used with the small-block, and this was the approach chosen for the staggered-valve big-block as well. The established engine length left substantial proportions for the crankshaft main bearings and connecting rod bearings.

The X- and Y-engine designs based on the small-block were replaced by

Before the driver was a sea of brightwork. Chrome and brushed aluminum were in abundance. On the dashboard is the optional electronic eye to dim the high-beam headlights automatically. The interior of this Impala featured a striking turquoise, black, and gray vinyl that contrasts beautifully with the gleaming black exterior.

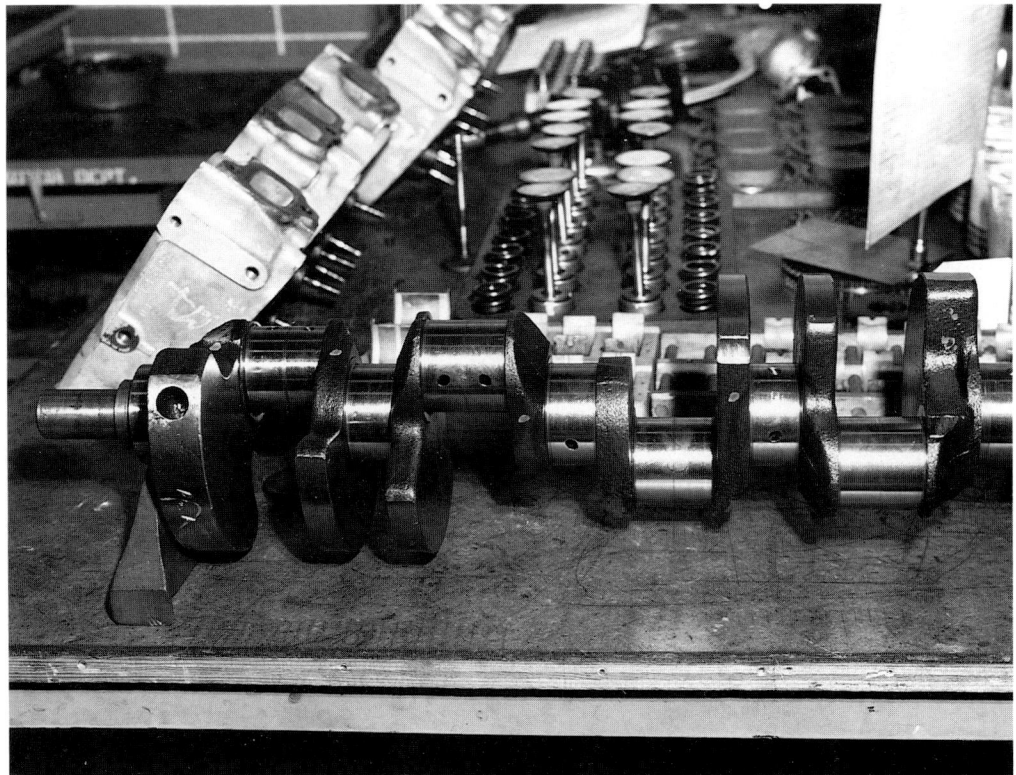

As with all Chevrolet engines, after durability testing, the 348ci V-8 was torn down and inspected for signs of wear. This is the 348 crankshaft with 2.4985in-diameter main bearing journals.

The chassis for the 1958 Chevrolet was completely new, with massive frame rails and cross-member. Here, the 348 is fitted to a pre-production chassis to check for proper clearances. The belt-driven compressor at the front of the engine is for the optional Level Air suspension.

designs with a larger, 4.84in bore center of various displacements, including 307ci, 348ci, and 369ci.

Richard L. Keinath was part of the original 348 design team. He graduated from Michigan State University in 1950 and went to work for the GM engineering staff. He transferred to the Chevrolet Division in 1952. Keinath was part of the engineering exodus in 1955 from downtown Detroit to the new Chevrolet Engineering Center in Warren, north of Detroit on Thirteen Mile Road. The new big-block V-8 was the first all-new engine designed at the sophisticated new facilities.

"I remember where we laid down the first line of that job at the Chevrolet Engineering Center: second floor, room 310, north end of the building," Keinath said. "Al Kolbe was the design engineer. Then, in drafting, there was John Devine, Fred Frincke, Dave Martens, myself, Denny Davis, Cal Wade, and probably Jack Roberts. Each of us got a part of the engine. Ed Durand got the crankshaft, Doug Armstrong had parts of the block, Fred Frincke did the intake manifold. I worked on the valvetrain—pushrods, valves, rocker arms—from the camshaft on up. This was all done by hand—no computers, just a slide rule.

"There were initially two displacements of the W-engine, a 307ci and a 348ci version. The bore and stroke on the 307ci W-engine was 3 7/8in by 3 1/4in. The 348ci engine was 4 1/8 by 3 1/4. The 307 never saw the light of day. By 1957, the 283ci small-block V-8 was so good that the 307ci W-engine didn't do anything for the car. It was a heavier engine, it didn't put out any more horsepower than the 283 would, so we dropped the 307 and went directly to the 348."

Combustion Chamber

To meet its second major objective—adaptability to a broad range of compression ratios to match future octane trends—the engineering staff chose a unique configuration for the combustion chamber. The engineers knew from Chevrolet's experience with the 283ci small-block V-8 that a new cylinder head had to be designed and tooled for each compression change. The authors of the 1958 SAE paper elaborated on the problems a single

cylinder head imposes on the manufacturer.

"It was obvious that with the combustion chamber placed in the cylinder head, it was necessary to retool at the foundry every time a compression ratio change is in order," wrote Rausch, Kehrl, and McPherson. "The necessity of making special heads to provide a range of compression ratios and to permit attachment of accessory mountings for the various model applications is of serious concern to the manufacturing and service departments. Chevrolet manufactures and services eight different heads for the 283 cubic inch engine because of the requirements imposed by multiple model usage. It would be possible to reduce this number of cylinder heads, but, to add the necessary tools and equipment to a previously established automated machine line, the cost becomes prohibitive, because generally the volume of production for special requirements is low."

This was the driving force behind the unorthodox cylinder head that finally emerged. After many meetings of the engineering staff and countless sketches and drawings, a design was settled on that left the cylinder head surface around the valves essentially flat, with the combustion chamber actually formed by the piston configuration within the bore at top dead center.

Although the SAE paper gave the official reasons for going to such a cylinder head and block concept, the impetus behind the design was on a more personal level. Dave Martens joined Chevrolet in 1952 after graduating from college, and spent the next two years going through the company's thorough training program. He worked in the drafting department on engines alongside Dick Keinath, Fred

The 348ci big-block V-8 did not announce its displacement on the valve covers. The valve cover shape was dictated by the intake and exhaust valves, configured in the shape of a W, and told gas jockeys all they needed to know. Note the position of the dual-snorkel air cleaner.

Frincke, and the others, all of whom would in the succeeding decades go on to make their mark in Chevrolet engine design.

"Al Kolbe was the design engineer in charge of this project," Martens said. "He was heavily influenced by Mercedes Benz's inline six-cylinder engine, which had a deck slanted off–not perpendicular to the bore centers. This was a 1952 Mercedes engine that won the Mexican Road Race in a 300 SL. That particular design influenced Kolbe in slanting the deck of the W-engine.

17

The 348ci V-8 was offered in four states of tune in 1958. The top powerplant was engine code 573B with a solid lifter camshaft and 3x2-barrel carburetion, rated at 315hp. Front and rear carburetors operated through a staged mechanical linkage.

"When I retired in 1987, I got a lamp made out of parts of engines I was associated with during my career. The shade of that lamp is a reproduction of a layout that I did of the combustion chamber, titled 'Combustion Chamber for W Engine–307 and 369 Cubic Inch Displacement,' which I started January 25, 1955, and completed February 17, 1956. Herbert G. Sood has written his signature on it as 'approved,' and Al Kolbe's signature is on the drawing, later in 1956.

"I had that to do with the initial design, and established, if not the final combustion chamber, the procedures

to design the combustion chamber to get the correct compression ratio. There was a lot of fooling around with the valve clearance notches in the cylinder block."

The SAE paper clearly spelled out the reasons, no doubt put forth by Kolbe, why the cylinder block and cylinder head should be configured the way they were. "Making the cylinder head with a flat bottom and placing the combustion chamber in the upper cylinder bore appeared to have possibilities of meeting the second objective [for the new V-8]," the engineers wrote. "Regardless of what changes might be made in piston shape, stroke, or bore size, the flat-bottom cylinder head would remain the same. It would also lend itself to freedom of valve shrouding to promote efficient flow characteristics. The actual combustion chamber shape could be achieved by contouring the piston head, by angling

the top of the block, or by a combination of both."

Essentially four requirements dictated the cylinder head and piston juxtaposition:

1. Compactness for fast burn rate.
2. A central spark position for minimum flame travel.
3. An adequate quench and squish area for turbulence.
4. The latitude to obtain different combustion volumes for a broad range of compression ratios, without affecting the piston shape or basic machining equipment.

The design that evolved was a cylinder block deck surface that was not perpendicular to the bore, but was inclined 16 degrees toward the intake side of the cylinder bank. The piston would have a gabled top surface with roughly one-half of the piston top parallel to the cylinder head surface; the other half of the piston–the exhaust

18

side—would combine with the cylinder block deck angle to produce a 32-degree angle. It was this resulting volume at top dead center that formed the combustion chamber. This volume could be decreased, and the resulting compression ratio increased, by altering the design of the piston. Changing the design of the piston to boost the compression ratio was far less expen-

sive than redesigning the entire cylinder head.

Before having to go to a new piston, however, the engineers could vary the compression ratio by means of milled cutouts in the combustion area of the cylinder bore. Two milled cutouts produced a 7.5:1 compression ratio; one milled cutout produced a 9.5:1 compression ratio. The elimina-

Subtle styling changes to the Impala for 1960 subdued the controversy generated by the 1959 model. Still no medallion or badge identified that a 348ci big-block V-8 was under the hood. Chevrolet

The 348ci V-8 was designed from the beginning to go in Chevrolet trucks as well as cars. It provided substantially more power and torque than the small-block V-8 for medium- and heavy-duty truck applications. This 1960 Spartan Model 80 with tilt-cab was new for that year. The shift and other controls were permanently mounted on the "island" above the engine and radiator. An access panel at the back of the cab allowed checking and replenishing the engine oil and coolant without raising the cab.

tion of this one cutout would boost the compression ratio even further. After this, a new piston design would give flexibility to raise the compression ratio if necessary.

The unique positioning of the intake and exhaust valves in the shape of a W led the engineers to refer to the new V-8 as the W-engine. The position of the valves also allowed advantageous positioning of the spark plug, resulting in good scavenging, a fast burn rate, and reduced oil fouling. Unlike those in the small-block V-8, the spark plugs were located above the exhaust manifold.

The cylinder head was designed to be used on either side of the engine, eliminating the need for left- and right-hand cylinder heads. The front and back of the cylinder head received the same three tapped holes for the mounting of the air conditioner and the Level Air compressors for passenger cars, and the air brake, air compressor, and power steering pump for trucks.

Development Program

With conception and initial design out of the way, Chevrolet moved quickly to produce the first prototype

348ci V-8 for developmental testing. A satisfactory development program was crucial to pinpoint trouble spots so that design revisions could be incorporated before commitments for long-lead production tooling could be ordered. Chevrolet engineering was concerned with three main questions, as stated in the 1958 SAE paper:

"1. Was the basic combustion chamber design satisfactory from the standpoint of specific power output, fuel octane requirement, and fuel economy?

The Impala received completely new styling for 1961. The most handsome body style was the two-door pillarless sport coupe. It was nicknamed the bubbletop for its tremendous glass area and rear visibility.

The Super Sport package introduced in 1961 made the Impala even sportier, with appearance and performance features that turned the car into a joy to drive. Exterior identification included SS badges on the rear quarter panels and on the center of the trunk lid.

"2. Would the location of the combustion chamber inside the cylinder block produce any special cooling problems requiring major tooling changes?

"3. Would the larger piston crown area resulting from the gabled head design increase piston temperatures and durability problems?"

The most crucial issue was cylinder head and block cooling, and this was tackled first. Testing with thermocouples and a unique Plexiglas plate bolted to the block deck surface revealed low coolant turbulence and resulting hot spots. Temperatures varied from 238 degrees Fahrenheit to

158 degrees Fahrenheit. The water pump inlet was moved to the outer portion of the cylinder banks, and coolant temperatures varied less than 10 degrees Fahrenheit. This design was adopted for the 348.

The brake mean effective pressure, minimum spark advance for best torque, leanest best torque fuel requirements, and crucial borderline knock characteristics revealed by dynamometer testing proved that the combustion chamber performance was satisfactory. This was a key concern because the performance requirements for passenger cars and trucks are very different.

The next key area targeted was piston durability. Preliminary testing showed that some modification of the gabled piston was required. The compression height–the distance from the piston pin center to the top of the piston–was increased 0.06in. The wall thickness of the piston, known as the ring belt thickness, was also increased 0.06in.

"At this time," the SAE paper stated, "it was felt that sufficient development work had been done to predict that the basic engine design would make a satisfactory product. This was also the point of no return insofar as the production tooling was concerned, as the basic production machinery was on order. If we made many major engineering changes from this point on, we would incur large cancellation charges and possibly find it impossible to meet production deadlines."

At this point, Kolbe had reservations about the W-engine's design.

"I don't know why Kolbe became so enamored of that particular design," Martens said. "My impression was, near the end of the design stages of that engine, he had second thoughts and would have liked to have reverted back to a deck face normal to the bores, but by that time, it was way too late because machine tools had been committed."

Despite the W-configuration of the intake and exhaust valves compared with their inline position on the small-block V-8, Chevrolet did not encounter any surprises during development testing. Late in the program, however, some valves cracked between the valve head and the tapered area of the stem.

Valve guide wear coupled with lifter leakdown was found to be the cause. This was solved by careful attention to the surface finish of the valve guide and improved lubrication of the valve stem. Also, the taper from the valve head to the stem was changed to add more material.

Durability Testing

Owing to the cost of the experimental prototype engine, Chevrolet installed numerous warning devices to sense impending destruction during durability testing. These instruments monitored excessive vibration, loss of torque, low oil pressure, high coolant temperature, and approaching redline. On a number of occasions, they shut down the test engine before damage resulted in the loss of a costly engine. At the same time, these incidences gave Chevrolet engineers valuable information regarding potential trouble spots so they could correct any design flaws.

Two types of durability testing took place to evaluate the reciprocating parts and the valvetrain. These included full-throttle tests to 4500 revolutions per minute (rpm) and a long-term cycle durability test from idle to partial throttle and finally full throttle.

"By the time construction of preproduction pilot line prototypes had begun," the engineers wrote in the 1958 SAE paper, "more than 40 experimental engine assemblies had been put through tests of varying length and severity, over a period of about 18 months. One of the engines built in our Engineering experimental shops had successfully completed a 200-hour wide-open throttle test at 4500 rpm–equivalent to 20,000 miles at 100 miles an hour. The 1,000-hour cycling durability test also had been run successfully.

"The pilot line prototype engines were built by the Tonawanda engine plant, using production tools wherever possible. The purpose of the test program using the pilot line engines was to determine whether any durability problems might develop as a result of variations from experimentally built engines to production engines."

These pilot line prototype engines were tested both at Tonawanda and at the Chevrolet Engineering Center. Testing revealed the need for minor changes to the engine block and cylinder head to correct for shift variations in the sand core at the foundry.

The final phase of testing was with the 348ci V-8 in the vehicles themselves, both cars and trucks, at the GM Proving Grounds in Milford, Michigan. Cumulative vehicle testing with the new engine exceeded 1 million miles.

With durability testing completed, Tonawanda commenced full production for the 1958 model year.

Technical Specifications

The 348ci Turbo-Thrust V-8 had a 4.125in bore and a 3.25in stroke, producing a very undersquare stroke-to-bore ratio of 0.79:1. The bore centers were 4.84in, a dimension that has remained common to every Chevrolet production big-block V-8. The crankshaft was forged steel, and the engine block used two-bolt main bearing caps in all applications. The main bearing diameter was 2.4985in. The crankpin journal diameter was 2in. The connecting rods were forged and had a center-to-center length of 6.135in, compared with the small-block connecting rod length of 5.7in. The intake valve diameter was 1.94in, and the exhaust valve diameter was 1.66in.

Four 348ci V-8s were available in cars. The first optional engine with a four-barrel carburetor and a 9.5:1 compression ratio was rated at 250 horsepower (hp) at 4400rpm and 355 pounds-feet (lb-ft) of torque at 2800rpm; the engine code was 576A. Next was the 573A, with a triple two-barrel carburetor setup and a 9.5:1 compression ratio, rated at 280hp at 4800rpm and 355lb-ft of torque at 3200rpm. The third offering was the 576B, with a four-barrel carburetor, a mechanical camshaft, and an 11:1 compression ratio, rated at 300hp at 5600rpm and 350lb-ft of torque at 3600rpm. The most powerful 348ci V-8 was the 573B option, with an 11:1 compression ratio, triple two-barrel carburetion, and a mechanical camshaft rated at 315hp at 5600rpm and 356lb-ft of torque at 3600rpm.

The hydraulic camshaft had an intake duration of 266 degrees, an exhaust duration of 274 degrees, and a

Included in the Super Sport package was a padded dash, a tachometer mounted on the steering column, and a passenger-side assist bar with Impala SS identification. The four-speed manual synchro-mesh transmission was standard with the Super Sport package.

valve overlap of 44 degrees, with intake and exhaust lifts of 0.3987in. The Automobile Manufacturers Association (AMA) specifications did not give the intake duration for the mechanical lifter camshaft, but the exhaust duration was 287 degrees and the valve overlap was 66 degrees, with an intake valve lift of 0.4058in and an exhaust valve lift of 0.412in.

Debut of the 348ci Turbo-Thrust V-8

The 348ci V-8 big-block wasn't all that was new for 1958. Chevrolet chose to restyle its cars completely. This was the era of the annual model change, and the 1958 car line exemplified that.

The taut, compact lines that distinguished the 1955, 1956, and 1957 models were abandoned for a longer, lower, and wider look. A new, top-of-the-line model, the Impala, was introduced.

In the April 1958 issue of *Motor Trend*, Chevrolet ran an advertisement for the new big-block: "New in the way it looks...in the way it feels–Chevy's Turbo-Thrust V-8!" The ad went on to say: "Here's an engineering achievement you can feel the instant your toe touches the treadle. You feel a new kind of response–an ultra-smooth pickup. And when you lift that Chevrolet hood you'll see why. You'll see an engine so radical it even *looks* different. It's the Turbo-Thrust V-8. It's built around a revolutionary design that contributes to constant smoothness at *all* engine speeds and to exceptional efficiency as well."

Car Life editor Jim Whipple tested a 283ci small-block V-8 and a 348ci big-block V-8 Chevrolet for the January 1958 issue of that magazine. "Performance of the new Chevy is very powerful," Whipple wrote. "Both the 283 and 348 engine will move the car along at 100 miles per hour with ease and are remarkably quiet.

"I had an excellent chance to compare the 'old' 283 cu. in. engine with the new 348 cu. in. plant on the 7 percent test grade. From a standing start the 283-engined Bel Air was hitting 70 mph at the top after a half-mile climb at full throttle. At the end of its climb the 348 cu. in. V-8 engined Impala, which tipped the scales at 150 lbs more, was doing an indicated 85 mph."

Prices? The Impala convertible, for example, listed for $2,841. The 250hp 348ci Turbo-Thrust V-8 was only $59 more. The 280hp 348ci Super Turbo-Thrust V-8 was a mere $70 more. (The dollar bought a lot back then.)

Plenty of changes were made for 1959. The restyled 1959 Chevrolet was the talk of the automotive press. As wild as the styling was, big-block fans wanted to know what modifications had taken place under the sleek new hood.

The number of optional 348s expanded from four to five, and Chevrolet clearly delineated the different types of big-block V-8s available in its 1959 brochure. First was the Turbo-Thrust V-8, Regular Production Op-

tion (RPO) 576A, with a 9.5:1 compression ratio and a four-barrel carburetor, rated at 250hp. Next came the Super Turbo-Thrust V-8, RPO 573A, with a 9.5:1 compression ratio and triple two-barrel carburetion, rated at 280hp. The Turbo-Thrust Special V-8, RPO 577, with an 11:1 compression ratio and a four-barrel carburetor, was rated at 320hp; the same engine gave 305hp with the two-speed Powerglide transmission, making it RPO 576B. Finally came the 335hp Super Turbo-Thrust Special, RPO 574, with an 11.25:1 compression ratio and triple two-barrel carburetion. The 315hp 348ci triple two-barrel V-8, RPO 573B, was dropped for 1959 but would return in 1960.

Three different 348ci Turbo-Thrust big-block V-8s were available within the Super Sport option for 1961: the 305hp four-barrel, the 340hp four-barrel, and the 350hp 3x2-barrel.

Prices skyrocketed for the optional big-block 348 V-8 in 1959. The 250hp Turbo-Thrust V-8 was now $199. The 280hp Super Turbo-Thrust V-8 was $269. In 1959, these were substantial sums.

Speed Age magazine tested the rakish 1959 Chevy Impala for its December 1958 issue. The car came with the 250hp 348ci big-block V-8, Turboglide automatic transmission, and

25

The 348ci W-engine was offered through 1961. That was the last year 3x2-barrel carburetion, or Tri-Power, was offered on a big-block until the 427ci V-8 made it available again in 1967.

3.08in rear axle. It reached 60 miles per hour (mph) in 10.7 seconds and covered the quarter-mile in 18.5 seconds, doing 80mph through the lights. The top speed was an indicated 123mph.

Engineers continued to work hard to make the W-engine breathe and generate more power. Dick Keinath re-

membered those efforts made in the late fifties. "Zora [Arkus-Duntov] was in charge of all high-performance V-8s, not just Corvettes," Keinath said. "The 348 was a bear to work on. We'd come up with what we thought were excellent ideas to make this engine really respond and put out horsepower, we built parts for it, installed them on the engine, and nothing worked, or very little. It just did not respond like the small-block. It was not as pleasant to work on as the small-block. The valves were more shrouded and the turns on the inlet port were more severe than [on the] the small-block. We had to do a lot of cam work on the engine."

Fred Frincke also remembered the performance development work he did on the 348. "I designed a cylinder head for Duntov for the 348ci big-block V-8," Frincke said. "We tried to improve the flow of the intake ports and the exhaust ports. We constructed models of intake ports and exhaust ports with valves in them of different shapes and sizes. We flow-tested these models on the carburetor flow bench at the Engineering Center. We applied different amounts of vacuum and valve lifts and plotted curves to see what flowed the best.

"We had a pattern shop at the Engineering Center. The patterns for the cylinder head casting would be made at the Engineering Center, and then the processor would decide where was the best place to get the sand mold made and get the experimental castings made. Sometimes it would be a foundry up in Saginaw, Michigan, or a foundry at GM Research, and in some cases, at Tonawanda."

These efforts bore fruit. The 348 performed admirably in circle track racing. The Daytona 500 was by far the most prestigious NASCAR event, and Junior Johnson won the 500 in 1960, racing the 348ci big-block V-8 and averaging 124.74mph.

The big-block offerings and ratings remained unchanged for 1960. Prices ranged from $188 for the 250hp Turbo-Thrust V-8 to $333 for the 335hp Super Turbo-Thrust Special V-8. The 320hp and 335hp versions were again only available with either the three-speed or four-speed synchromesh manual transmissions. The hottest 348 available with automatic transmission was the 305hp four-barrel version, RPO 576, with the heavy-duty two-speed Powerglide transmission.

Roger Huntington tested the mechanical cam 305hp 348 with the Powerglide transmission and 3.55 rear axle ratio in an Impala four-door for the March 1960 issue of *Motor Life*.

"Acceleration performance was very satisfactory—really 'neck-snapping' in fact," Huntington wrote. "When you tromp it from a standing start the car jumps off the line with a sudden surge of low-end torque—but with a minimum of nose lifting, due to the anti-squat linkage in the rear suspension. It takes only 4.8 secs. to get from 30 to 60 mph, giving an overall 0–60 time of 8.4 [secs.]. I've always thought the sensation of acceleration was greatly affected by other senses like sound and sight. This police Chev scores high here. Just to see that front end heel over several degrees to the right from engine torque reaction does something to you!"

The 348ci V-8 was offered in passenger cars for the last time in 1961, although it continued in production for trucks and the export market through 1965. Some reshuffling of the 348 took place in 1961. The 250hp (RPO 576A), 280hp (RPO 573A), and 305hp (RPO 576B) engines continued. The 320hp four-barrel V-8, RPO 577, was dropped, replaced by the 340hp four-barrel 348, RPO 590. The top of the 348 line was the 350hp triple two-barrel version, RPO 573B, a $365 option.

The automotive world was swarming with rumors of a new, bigger big-block that Chevrolet was to announce. Later in the 1961 model year, the 409ci V-8 was written up in the enthusiast magazines, but the new W-engine was not yet in full production. The few cars that were built with it in 1961 were meant to stir the pot, and they succeeded.

The ground-breaking 348ci big-block V-8 had served Chevrolet Division well for its four short years in passenger cars. With the release of the new 409ci V-8, it all too quickly became a memory.

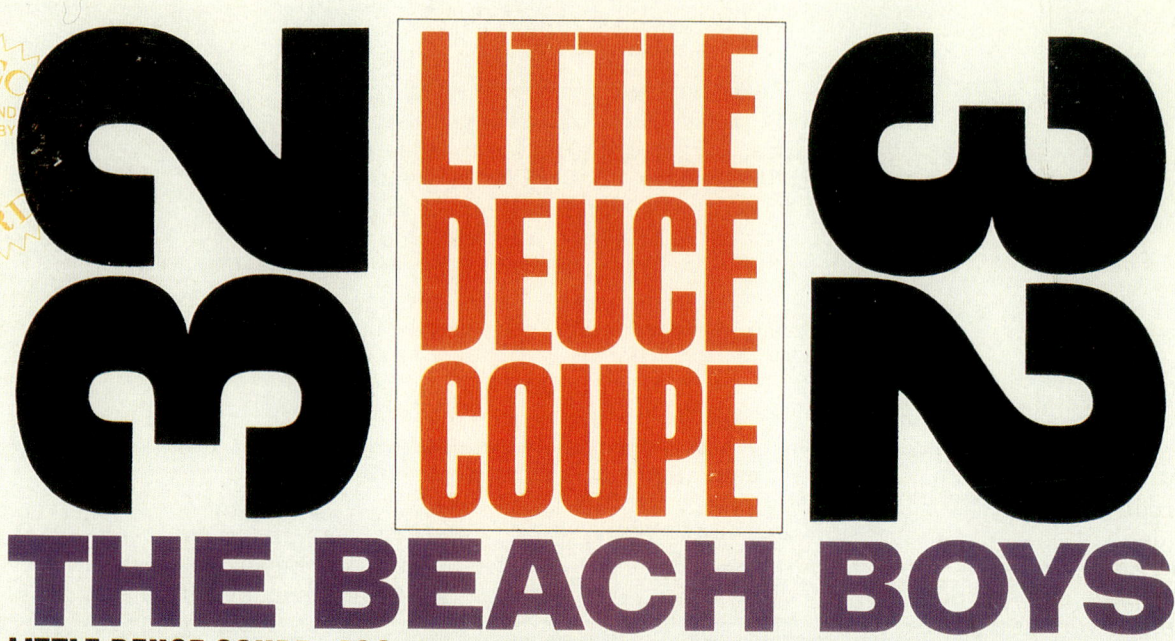

Chapter 2

The 409

The Engine That Inspired a Song

The W-engine seemed to be a good engine for drag
racing. It was more successful in the drags than
it was on the oval tracks.

–Fred Frincke

Chevrolet introduced the 409ci V-8 in 1961 in a deliberate effort to increase significantly the performance of the W-engine. It upgraded the powerplant in response to a number of pressures. For one, the general trend in the industry was toward larger-displacement V-8s as cars got longer, lower, wider, and in many cases heavier. It was natural to meet or beat the competition—other car companies—in terms of displacement. In addition, sanctioned competition in stock car and drag racing practically screamed for more cubic inches and power.

Zora Arkus-Duntov was quite aggressive in his performance development of the 348. Much work had been done in the areas of camshafts—both hydraulic and mechanical—as well as carburetion and compression ratios. Duntov was not able to get dual four-barrel carburetors put on the 348, as he had on the small-block V-8; three two-barrel carburetors was the top multiple-carburetion setup. Consider-

The Beach Boys became synonymous with car songs in the early sixties, and one of the most famous car songs ever written was "409." The album containing this song sold more than 1 million copies almost overnight. Capitol Industries

Chevrolet decided to let gas jockeys know the displacement of the newest W-engine, starting with the 409ci V-8. Chromed valve covers and air cleaner were rare dress-up options.

ing that Chevrolet billed itself as "the leader in the low-priced field," the buyer got a lot of performance for the money with the 348.

During discussions with other engineers shortly after the 348 was released, however, it was clear to Duntov, General Manager Ed Cole, and others, that a displacement increase was inevitable. To get an engine that breathed better, which was the key to more power, they needed larger bores to accommodate larger valves. Chevrolet wasted little time doing that, and released the new W-engine to rave reviews.

The 409—She's Real Fine

The release of the 409 had the desired effect, both on the consumer and in competition circles. Everyone, it seemed, agreed that the 409ci V-8 was one hot engine, regardless of what form it came in. The numbers 4-0-9 were magic, and rolled off the tongue of bow-tie enthusiasts with reverence. Chevrolet's largest V-8 quickly eclipsed the 348. The two engines co-existed for 1961, but then the 348 was dropped at the end of the model year.

The 409 became the hot ticket, both on the quarter-mile strip and for cruising the streets. The engine's performance through the timing lights

The 409ci V-8 was introduced in 1961. It featured a larger, 4.31in bore and longer, 3.5in stroke. The intake valve diameter was 2.06in, and the exhaust valve diameter was 1.72in. The main bearing and connecting rod bearing diameters of 2.5in and 2.2in, respectively, remained unchanged. The only 409ci V-8 available in 1961 was equipped with a four-barrel carburetor and was rated at 360hp. In 1962, Chevrolet offered a complete line of 409ci V-8s, replacing the 348ci V-8.

and from stoplight to stoplight became legendary. It fired the imagination of enthusiasts everywhere, but nowhere was the flame hotter than in California.

Trends of almost any nature began in California, and this was particularly true of music. The Beach Boys burst upon the scene in 1962 with their hit "Surfin' U.S.A." The group tapped into the California mood by singing about the adolescent preoccupation with surfing, cars, and girls. It established a musical genre, and opened the floodgates to imitators, both good and bad.

When it came to singing about cars, the Beach Boys had no equal, except perhaps for Jan and Dean. One of the first songs ever written about a V-8 engine, if not *the* first, was "409," created by Brian Wilson, leader of the Beach Boys, and Gary Usher. It was about a boy who had saved his money for a car long before he knew there would be a 409ci Chevrolet, and how the 409 he eventually bought was the fastest car at the drag strip, all sung to the accompaniment of a car engine revving in the background at the appropriate times.

The song struck a nerve and became a Top Ten hit. It was included on the album *Little Deuce Coupe*, which sold more than a million copies. The album was an ode to youth's love affair with the automobile. Besides the title

cut and "409," it featured "Shut Down," "Spirit of America," "Our Car Club," and other automotive tunes.

Chevrolet couldn't have hoped for more. "409" was played countless times, over hundreds of radio stations

The 409ci V-8 was introduced late in 1961. Only 142 were sold in Impalas that year, as Chevrolet made refinements for full-fledged production in 1962. This 1961 Impala SS is one of the few remaining.

Unlike the pistons used in the 348ci V-8, those used in all 409ci V-8s were forged, or "impact extruded," in GM parlance.

The difference between the car and truck versions of the 409 are subtle but visible in these two cross-section photos. The automotive 409 features a low-profile air cleaner, and the dipstick is on the left, or driver, side of the engine. The piston at top dead center shows less combustion chamber volume, producing a higher compression ratio.

across the country, amounting to saturation advertising that didn't cost Chevrolet a dime. Did the song spark sales? To be sure, it did, but no one knew to what degree. It was a moot point: The performance image of the new W-engine was firmly established.

Technical Specifications

The 409's displacement was achieved by increasing the 348's bore to 4.3125in and stroke to 3.5in. To get such a dramatic bore increase, changes to the sand cores used for casting the block had to be made to maintain adequate bore wall thickness. The machined valve cutouts in the combustion chamber of the high-performance large-valve 348s were eliminated with the 409. The larger, heavier counterweights necessitated by the longer stroke required changes to the lower block for proper reciprocating clearance.

Only one 409ci V-8 was offered in 1961, introduced midyear. It was rated at 360hp at 5800rpm and, interestingly, 409lb-ft of torque at 3600rpm, running with a single four-barrel carburetor. Numerous published sources, including road tests, gave the engine's compression ratio as 11.25:1. The "1961 Chevrolet Advertised Engine Ratings" for passenger cars and the Corvette, dated December 30, 1960, and signed by Maurice S. Rosenberger, however, gave a compression ratio of 11:1. The engine's RPO number was 580.

The camshaft was mechanical. The intake valve diameter was a nominal 2.065in; the exhaust valve diameter was a nominal 1.72in.

This 360hp 409 came with a cast-aluminum intake manifold. The four-barrel carburetor was a Carter AFB unit with 1.625in-diameter primary throttle bores and 1.6875in-diameter secondary throttle bores. The venturi diameter was 1.34in on the primaries and 1.56in on the secondaries.

Only 142 Impalas in Super Sport trim with the optional 409ci V-8 were built in 1961. *Motor Trend* tested the new big-block 409 Impala SS for its September 1961 issue. "Put the big 409-cubic-inch engine into the new Super Sport package and you have one of the hottest test cars of the season. *MT* checks it out from its design features to its drag strip potential," the editors wrote.

Immediately, the 409 was identified as a drag strip car, and this image would remain throughout the engine's entire four-year production life for passenger cars. Although several years passed before the 348ci V-8 could claim a respectable performance image, the 409 achieved that goal the moment the enthusiast magazines got their hands on an example to test.

There was a reason for this. Chevrolet made a deliberate effort to imbue the 409 with a performance image from the moment of its introduction, to overcome the less-than-sterling performance image of the 348.

It backed this up with real numbers in terms of output and quarter-mile performance times and kept improving them with each new year. The car maker had enough standard engines for its cars: the straight six, the 283ci small-block V-8, and the 348ci V-8 in its last year of production. Along with the numbers, it advertised the 409's prowess, and it kept hammering these qualities home.

The enthusiast magazines also beat the drum regarding the performance of the 409. *Motor Trend* tested the 360hp Impala SS with a limited-slip differential and two rear axle ratios. Equipped with a 3.36 rear axle, the car reached 60mph in 7.8 seconds, and covered the quarter-mile in 15.31 seconds doing 94.24mph. With the dealer-installed 4.56 rear gears, the car reached 60mph in 7 seconds, and achieved an elapsed time (ET) of 14.02 seconds doing 98.14mph.

Even though the 409 was a midyear introduction, it helped Chevrolet carve out the lion's share of the National Hot Rod Association (NHRA) wins in 1961. Of the fifty-three NHRA classes that year, Chevys won twenty-seven, Fords only four.

For 1962, the 348ci V-8 was dropped from the list of passenger car options, replaced by two 409ci V-8s. The RPO 580 four-barrel V-8 received 20 more horsepower to run at 360hp, and a new dual four-barrel 409, RPO 587, with 409hp was added to the line. With these engines, Chevrolet dropped the Turbo-Thrust descriptive adjective and adopted Turbo-Fire, as used with the small-block V-8.

In actual numbers, the four-barrel 409 was rated at 380hp at 5800rpm and 420lb-ft of torque at 3200rpm. It was a $428 option. The dual four-barrel 409 was rated at 409hp at 6000rpm and 420lb-ft of torque at 4000rpm. Both engines ran an 11:1

The truck version of the 409ci V-8 had a much taller air cleaner, the oil dipstick was mounted on the right side and toward the front of the engine for easier access, and the cross section of the piston shows a completely different configuration. Coolant passages in the truck version differed from those in the passenger car version and featured steam holes between the cylinder block and head. Even the spark plugs were different.

Next page
The bubble-top styling of the 1961 Impala sport coupe was not only attractive, it was the choice of drag racers who began to campaign the 409. Starting that year, Chevrolet began to mount displacement badges on the front fenders, with crossed flags bearing the Chevrolet coat of arms and the checkered flag of victory.

compression ratio. The dual four-barrel option cost $484. Truly, the 409/409 was designed with the NHRA in mind. The performance increase was due primarily to new, larger-port cylinder heads with 2.19in-diameter intake valves; the exhaust valve diameter remained at 1.72in.

Both engines ran the same solid lifter camshaft. The AMA specifications give an intake duration of 398 degrees and an exhaust duration of 353 degrees. The intake duration is not a misprint. According to procedures at the time, these were the numbers generated for use in the AMA specifications. Later, more realistic calculations were adopted, and real-world specifications generated. Intake and exhaust valve lifts were 0.4396in.

The carburetor on the 380hp 409 varied depending on the transmission chosen. With a three-speed manual

transmission, the engine received Carter four-barrel model number 3820580, which had 1.625in primaries and 1.687in secondaries. Four-speed–equipped engines got Rochester model number 7020028, which had 1.562in primaries and 1.687in secondaries.

The dual four-barrel 409 used two Carter units for both three-and four-speed manual transmissions. The front carburetor was model number 3815403, and the rear carburetor was model number 3815404. Both carburetors had 1.562in primaries and 1.687in secondaries.

The 409 was quickly becoming *the* power to be reckoned with at the drag strip. The names of men like Dave Strickler driving the Bill Jenkins–tuned *Old Reliable II* campaigned by Ammon R. Smith Auto Company of York, Pennsylvania, be-

Before the era of bucket seats, the wide bench seat allowed the owner of this 409 to have his sweetheart sit next to him. Note the grab bar on the passenger side, which was part of the Super Sport package. The tachometer that came as part of the Super Sport package was not redlined, but nevertheless helped drivers pick their shift points and avoid overrevving.

came household words among Chevy car club members. Other notables entered the racing lexicon under the Chevy banner: Don Nicholson and Hayden ("Mr. 409") Proffit.

Upping the Ante

In 1963, Chevrolet dropped the number designation for its engines and adopted alphanumeric designations. Three 409ci V-8s were offered for this year. The L33 was a hydraulic

The dual four-barrel 409ci V-8, RPO L80, was the most powerful engine of the 409 series. Producing 425hp, it made Chevrolets among the hottest cars on the street and was the engine of choice for such drag racers as Hayden Proffit and Don Garlits.

A fully dressed L80 409ci V-8 ready for installation in 1963. This engine marked the zenith of high-performance development in the 409. Note the streamlined cast-iron exhaust manifold that contributed to the engine's output.

camshaft four-barrel with a 10:1 compression ratio, rated at 340hp at 5000rpm and 420lb-ft of torque at 3200rpm. Next was the L31, running a mechanical camshaft and a four-barrel carburetor, with an 11:1 compression ratio; it was rated at 400hp at 5800rpm and 425lb-ft of torque at 3600rpm. The option cost of the L31 was $428. The highest-output 409 designed to run on the street was the L80. This beast carried the now-familiar dual four-barrel carburetor setup with a stiff mechanical camshaft and an 11:1 compression ratio and was rated at 425hp at 6000rpm and 425lb-ft of torque at 4200rpm. The cost of the L80 was $484—an increase in performance with no increase in price over the previous year's. Inflation didn't exist in the early sixties!

Car Life magazine found the 340hp 409 a perfectly fine performer on the street. Wrote the editors: "The engine in our test car develops more torque than the 425 hp model over the speed range most use, i.e. from 500 to about 3500 rpm. Stated another way, the high torque 409/340 engine's advantage extends from 10 to 80 mph and at any speed in between it will have more punch than the 409/425 engine.

"As a matter of fact," the editors enthused, "there is so much torque that punching the throttle wide open at 40 mph will produce a very inspiring screech from the driving wheels and the car will literally leap ahead like the Impala for which it was named."

With the standard 3.36 rear axle and two-speed Powerglide transmission, the 340hp 409 Impala SS reached 60mph in 6.6 seconds, and covered the quarter-mile in 15.2 seconds doing 90mph through the lights. Not bad for a car with a curb weight of nearly 2 tons! Crucial to the car's acceleration was the optional Positraction. For around $3,500, the buyer had a very enjoyable car.

With such high-performance engines as Chevrolet's 409, the early sixties marked the dawn of the factory drag cars. Limited numbers of these vehicles were available for drag racing, and they carried not only modified engines, but modified bodies and chas-

sis as well. In 1963, Chevrolet introduced its factory drag car.

The Z-11

Aluminum front end sheet metal was available on 1962 Chevrolets with the dual four-barrel 409s, for drag racers wanting a lighter car. Chevrolet carried the drag racing concept further in 1963 and offered a larger-displacement W-engine with 427ci, having the RPO Z-11. The engineer in charge of the engine design was Fred Frincke.

"The Z-11 was a stroked 409," said Frincke. "We increased the stroke from 3.5in to 3.65in. I was assigned to [Zora Arkus-] Duntov working on the Z-11 at the same time Dick Keinath was designing the Mk II Mystery Engine. I worked on the intake mani-

folds, the cylinder heads, and the valley cover arrangement. So, I was still giving the last ounce of blood to the old-style engine to save it. It had a high-rise intake manifold, a special cylinder head with a step machined in it where the inlet manifold bolted on. The engine had a separate tappet valley cover. We had it set up such that you could remove the intake manifold without opening up the engine. You didn't have to disturb the distributor or the timing, and you didn't have to drain the water or remove the thermostat. We had two intake manifolds—a dual four-barrel and a single four-barrel—and you could change from one to the other in a short amount of time.

"I have a letter that was written by Paul Prior of Product Promotion

The 409ci V-8 introduced in 1961 came with a four-barrel carburetor, a solid lifter camshaft, and an 11:1 compression ratio, and was rated at 360hp. It immediately established a level of performance and image Chevrolet needed both on the street and on the strip.

Engineering in 1977 in answer to a query. He said there were fifty-seven Z-11 cars built. These were 1963 Impala SSs with aluminum bumpers and [an] aluminum front end. The Z-11 was advertised at 430hp. The W-engine seemed to be a good engine for racing. It was more successful in the drags than it was on the oval tracks."

The longer-stroke crankshaft was obviously new. Also new were the con-

NHRA rules permitted dual four-barrel carburetors, and Chevrolet made sure the 409 had them. This is the 409hp 409.

necting rods, pistons with a 12.5:1 compression ratio, and high-port cylinder heads with a matching intake manifold. The camshaft lift was a whopping 0.511in. The advertised horsepower was 430, but realistically, the engine dynoed at closer to 500.

Included in the $1,237.40 Z-11 option were the 430hp 427ci V-8, four-speed synchromesh transmission, 4.11 Positraction axle, metallic brake linings, heavy-duty shock absorbers and

springs, tachometer, aluminum hood and underhood panels, aluminum front fenders and inner panels, and aluminum front and rear bumpers. The Z-11's shipping weight was 3,345 pounds. By comparison, the curb weight of the standard Impala two-door with the 340hp 409 was 3,877 pounds.

The Z-11 had another distinguishing feature: it sported a new cowl air induction air cleaner, which provided cool, higher-pressure air to the engine, which boosted performance. This development was the result of testing conducted by Vince Piggins and is a story unto itself.

Big-Block Cowl Air Induction

In May of 1977, Vince Piggins wrote to this author describing his pioneering efforts regarding cowl induction in a paper titled "Carburetion Cold Air Induction." The research testing it discussed was performed on a 409, and it had far-reaching effects on both racing cars and passenger cars.

"For almost as long as internal combustion engines have been tested," Piggins wrote, "the effect of atmospheric conditions on engine performance has been a consideration. By using air temperatures, humidity, and barometric pressures as a correction factor, performance computations and volumetric efficiency of an engine may be compared over weeks of testing under changing conditions. The effect of air temperature on engine power is well known by all who are but only remotely mechanical.

"I have been unable to find any evidence prior to tests run by Chevrolet in July of 1962, where intentional use of reduced carburetor air temperatures was made in a stock passenger automobile to produce a performance increase. There have been numerous race cars having exposed carburetor ram tubes contained in a box or a form of scoop for ram effect, but none with the intent for reduced air temperature. Having made this statement, I am sure it will be immediately disputed.

"In a test program conducted at Daytona Speedway in July of 1962, a Chevrolet Biscayne 409 and a Pontiac 380 were compared to determine why the Pontiac was 1 1/2 to 2 miles per hour faster than the Chevrolet with 25 less horsepower. An engine switch was made and the Pontiac was faster using the Chevrolet engine which at least confirmed our original power findings.

"In conducting these tests, complete underhood environmental conditions were monitored in numerous locations giving us temperature and pressure readings in various locations, including the cowl plenum area that provides fresh air to the passenger compartment. Digesting and comparing the Chevrolet/Pontiac data, it was immediately evident that conditions within the Pontiac engine compartment were both lower in temperature and slightly higher pressure-wise in the immediate air cleaner area.

"To simulate this condition at the carburetor, an air scoop was fashioned from an extra flywheel housing cover, and attached to the Chevy hood over a hole connecting to the carburetor intake. This modification immediately increased the Chevy's top speed by 3 1/2 to 4 miles per hour per lap. Air pressure at the carburetor was raised to a level comparable to that of the Pontiac. The big change, however, was the carburetor air temperature being lowered from a previous 124 degrees [Fahrenheit] to 89 degrees, or a 35 degree overall temperature reduction. It was immediately evident that the com-

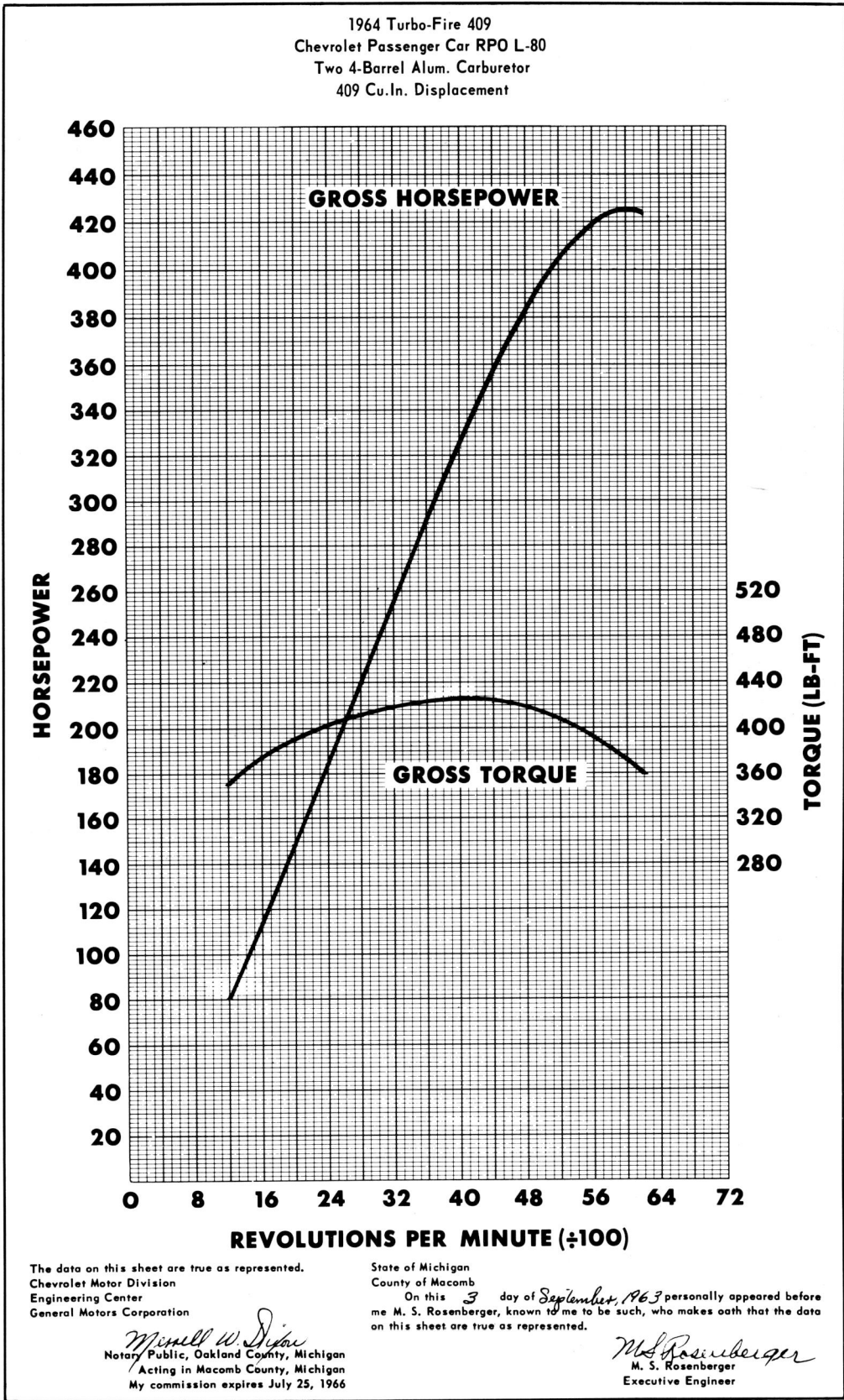

The horsepower and torque curves of the L80. This engine developed 425hp at 6000rpm and 425lb-ft of torque at 4000rpm. The chart is signed by Maurice S. Rosenberger, executive engineer.

The Z-11 was the first Chevrolet factory drag car with its own RPO. It was introduced in 1963 and included a 427ci W-series V-8. The newly developed cowl plenum intake was also used by the Mk IIS Daytona Mystery Engine. Musclecar Review

Next page
It took insight in 1965 to recognize a future collectible car, but the 409 Impala SS convertible definitely qualified. In its last year of production, the 409 shared the big-block limelight with the new 396ci Mk IV V-8.

plaint by many stock car drivers of being unable to maintain a lap speed within one or two miles per hour of their first qualifying lap [sic]. Obviously with underhood air intake, as the engine compartment temperatures rose, the speed and power decreased.

"Rex White and Louie Clemens (now a G.M. employee) were the driver/mechanic team doing these test series for Chevrolet on this warm July day. Doug Roe, an engineer with Chevrolet and working for Vince Piggins in the Product Performance Group at Warren, Michigan, was assigned to the test program.

"Roe was elated in reporting the news to Piggins of the 4 miles per hour gain in speed achieved. Armed with the data of the Daytona tests, Piggins reported to his Engineering management and suggested the immediate design, release and build of a special edition hood for the 1963 Chevrolet Biscayne. This was not to be, however, as major sheet metal changes are extremely expensive and require months of design and lead time to procure.

"The suggestion was made that in lieu of a new hood with air scoop, we consider tapping the abundant supply of fresh cooler air that was available in the cowl ventilator area of the vehicle. A special air cleaner for the Biscayne was designed and tested in October of 1962. The first race application of the new plenum chamber/carburetor air intake was concurrent with the introduction of Chevrolet's revolutionary Mk II mystery engine at the Daytona 500 in February 1963."

Although Piggins did not mention it in his paper, the cowl induction used on the Daytona Mystery Engine was also adopted for the Z-11.

Jet-Smooth Luxury for 1964

For 1964, Chevrolet refined the bodylines laid down by the 1963 model, and 1964-model Super Sports remain among some of the most handsome Chevrolets of the sixties.

The 409ci V-8 offerings–the 340hp L33, the 400hp L31, and the 425hp L80–all continued unchanged for 1964. One reason for this was the engineering effort being poured into the forthcoming big-block V-8 patterned

40

Top-down driving was the only way to travel with this car. For a fortunate few, it still is.

after the Mystery Engine that had been raced at the 1963 Daytona 500. Despite Chevrolet's ability in extracting horsepower from the 409ci W-engine, the engineers and drafters at Chevrolet Engineering Center were hard at work on the next-generation big-block V-8.

The showroom brochure for the new models read: "'64 Chevrolet...new looks in a great new Jet-smooth luxury lineup." Prices for the cars and engines remained virtually unchanged for 1964—something that does not occur today. The total number of Chevrolets built with the 409 was

8,684; most of these were Super Sports.

One of Chevrolet's most clever and eye-catching advertisements appeared in 1964, with the opener, "If You Like Playing with Blocks, Try This." The photo shows a 1964 Impala convertible, in front of which are the key high-performance parts of the 425hp 409, including the cylinder heads, pistons, connecting rods, camshaft, crankshaft, carburetor, and deep oil pan, with the bare engine block on an engine stand.

The End of an Era

The last production year for the 409ci V-8 was 1965. In several respects, the final version may be the most desirable of all 409s, because the Impala had completely new, sleek fastback styling; the 409 had a shortened production year owing to the imminent introduction of the new big-block; and this was the last year of 409 production in passenger cars.

Only 2,828 409-powered Chevrolets were built in 1965. The 340hp L33 was a $242.10 option, and the 400hp L31 cost $320.65. The 425hp L80 was dropped for 1965.

Car and Driver tested one of the last production 409 Impalas for its December 1964 issue, stating, "The beast of drag strip hollow has been transformed into a svelte beauty."

The car the editors put through its paces was an Impala SS with the 340hp V-8, the venerable Powerglide transmission, and a 3.31 axle. This was a good street setup, but not one to challenge high-performance cars on the track. Still, it reached 60mph in 8 seconds and covered the quarter-mile in 16.4 seconds.

"The 409 SS is a good automobile," the editors wrote, "especially for the

The 340hp 409ci four-barrel V-8 was the milder of the two 409s offered in 1965. Nevertheless, it delivered plenty of torque and impressive acceleration in the big Impala.

man who likes to run very fast on the big turnpikes. And with 41,000 miles of Interstate highways criss-crossing the United States, that can mean a lot of satisfying time behind the wheel."

Despite the shortcomings of the W-series engines, the 409 was one of Chevrolet's best powerplants, but it holds that status for reasons beyond engineering refinements. It captured a mood in America, defined a new performance level for Chevrolet, and actually established a mystique around itself. That mystique exists to this day, and when those immortal numbers 409 are spotted on the front fender at Chevy meets, they never fail to produce smiles of admiration.

Chapter 3

The 396/402

The Mk IV Big-Block V-8 Is Born

I can remember after we had run one of those engines enough to know it put out about 100 more horsepower than any 348 or 409 we ever had on the dynamometer…

–Maurice S. ("Rosy") Rosenberger

The sixties were a dynamic decade for automotive engineering. Government regulations were virtually nonexistent, and car companies had free rein to design and build practically any engine or automobile they desired–and the market wanted. Horsepower was sovereign, and automotive styling became the stuff not just of dreams, but of reality. The dollar was strong and still backed by silver until 1965; inflation was low, as were car prices. Buyers got a lot of car for the money.

The 409 had given Chevrolet's performance image a shot in the arm. The inherent design of the W-engine, however, precluded the standard procedures that made the 409 a power to be dealt with. It was not easy to make the 409 really breathe and produce the power to win routinely in NASCAR. Why was it important to win races, or even to compete at all? It is a concept

The 427ci Mystery Engine raced at the 1963 Daytona 500 was the basis of the Mk IV engine series. The splayed valve configuration of the cylinder head earned it the nickname "porcupine head." With tongue firmly in cheek, Chevrolet released this photo of the 425hp 396ci Turbo-Jet V-8 with its namesake–stuffed, to be sure–atop the air cleaner.

The Camaro received the Mk IV 396ci big-block in 1967. This subdued identification was the only indication of the displacement under the hood.

as old as the automobile itself: Racing improves the breed. In addition, an intangible link connects winning races and winning sales.

The engineers at Chevrolet knew all of this, and they also knew they needed a new engine to accomplish

their goal. That new engine–a *racing* engine–needed an advocate. The timing was fortuitous because Ed Cole moved up from being Chevrolet's general manager to being its corporate group vice-president in 1962. Semon E. ("Bunkie") Knudsen of Pontiac Division was selected by GM management to be Chevrolet's new general manager. Knudsen, aware of the high-stakes game of winning races and selling cars, became the force behind the new engine Chevrolet needed to win big in circle track racing. His decision to approve funding for the Mk II engine project was instrumental in the creation of the Mk IV street engine, with ramifications that are felt by big-block enthusiasts to this day.

The Mystery Engine

Many of the design parameters of the new racing engine were adopted almost line for line with those of the Mk IV V-8. Don McPherson, who was assistant staff engineer at the time, distinctly recalled how the highly secretive project got started:

"Bunkie Knudsen had just come in as general manager, and [Ed] Cole had gone on to group vice-president. Now, Bunkie didn't like the W-engine. He wanted an engine that would win Daytona. I was assistant staff engineer

Don McPherson had been involved with the design of the Chevrolet small-block V-8 and was assistant staff engineer at the time of the Mk IV engine project. He convinced the GM executive committee of the need to replace the 409ci W-series engine with a new design that offered better breathing.

and Jack Rausch was staff engineer of engines at the time. The assignment from Knudsen was to build an engine that would win Daytona and sell it to the corporation. He asked us, 'Could we win Daytona with that engine?' and I told him no, we couldn't, because of the restrictions in it. It didn't breathe very well, and the combustion chamber was not very good. And he said, 'Well, design me one that will do it.' And I thought to myself, 'You mean, we've got to sink the W after only being in production two or three years?' But we did it. That's how that engine got started."

Chevrolet had been adhering to the spirit, if not the letter, of the AMA ban of direct involvement by car companies in racing activities. Nevertheless, it was no surprise that all the car companies were giving indirect support in terms of research, development, and parts to private teams. This was a matter of self-preservation. No car company wanted to see its cars lose consistently, because that would have a dampening effect on the image of the cars in the marketplace.

Some engineers at Chevrolet already were less than satisfied with the W-engine, although Cole thought it was perfectly adequate for passenger cars and trucks. The idea of designing and building a new V-8 to replace the W had to be put forth, but certainly, racing could not be the reason for developing such an engine. In the mind of Knudsen and McPherson, pragmatic engineering and marketing reasons for creating a new V-8 engine had to be presented in the context of passenger cars and trucks if funding was to be granted. It was a closely guarded secret that the first steps in such an engine would take it to Daytona.

The task of getting approval for this new V-8 fell to McPherson. "I had the job of selling the corporation on the fact that Mr. Cole's engine—the W-engine from engineering staff—was no good and had to be replaced by the Mark engine," McPherson recalled. "I had to go before the engineering staff

Semon Knudsen became Chevrolet general manager in 1962. He was the dynamic mover behind the highly secretive Mk II racing engine, which was the basis for the production Mk IV big-block V-8 released in 1965. Here he poses with the new 1965 Chevelle Malibu SS396 with RPO Z-16. Only 201 Z-16s were built that year.

Next page
Perhaps the best showcase for the new 396ci big-block V-8 was the 1965 Corvette. Only 2,157 big-block Corvettes were built that year.

This cutaway illustration of the 325hp version of the 396ci V-8, RPO L35, reveals the ribbed floor of the dual-plane intake manifold to aid fuel distribution, and the splayed valves as originally designed for the Daytona 500 Mystery Engine. The intricate passages in the cylinder head were designed to keep the intake and exhaust valves cool.

and the executive committee downtown, including the president and chairman of GM, at the GM building and sell this thing. We pretty much stated the facts as to the problems

with breathing on the W and with surface-to-volume in the combustion chamber. The thing made engineering sense, and everybody bought it. It took about half an hour."

The task of engineering this powerplant was given to Dick Keinath. He clearly remembered the sequence of events that led to the engine to replace the already aging WV-8:

"Between 1958 and 1960, I was working for [Zora Arkus-]Duntov on the V-8s, including the 348. I worked for McPherson between 1960 and 1967. When I went to work for McPherson, I had been working on the

aluminum V-8 engine for Duntov. In 1961, I was working as the design engineer on the four- and six-cylinder engines but I also had responsibility for certain parts of the V-8s. The chief engineer at the time was Harry Barr. If Knudsen wanted to know about engines, he would call McPherson. He wouldn't go to Barr, then [Maurice] Rosenberger, and then McPherson. He would pick up the phone and call whomever he knew.

"Now, McPherson was very astute. He would cover with Rosenberger and Barr what Knudsen had said. After he hung up the phone, he would go in and

48

tell them, 'Hey, I just had a call from Knudsen, and you should be aware of what he said.' One day, I was called into Rosenberger's office. McPherson was sitting there, and I think Harry Barr was there too. They had been discussing the new engine Knudsen had requested. Now, be aware that this did not get above Knudsen—ever. Nobody above Knudsen in the corporation knew what was going on. This was the initial approach, and we didn't have much time to do it."

When Keinath began work on the Mk II, production feasibility was kept uppermost. Although this new engine

Power, speed, and beauty were all embodied in the 1965 Corvette with its first big-block V-8. On the open road, you can almost hear the theme music to "Route 66."

This partially machined 396ci big-block reveals the massive firewalls and pan rails that helped give the Mk IV great strength.

This inherent strength would later prove itself with the 500hp-plus L88 and ZL-1 427ci V-8s to follow.

This Mk IV–series bare block is bolted to a test fixture at the Chevrolet Engineering Center in 1966. Passenger car blocks had a

deck height of 9.8in. Truck blocks had a deck height of 10.2in to allow for taller pistons having an additional oil control ring.

would be designed to go racing, it would carry no exotic hardware like that developed by Duntov's group, which did research and development on high-performance engines, both small-block and big-block. The Mk II would be given no overhead camshafts, hemispherical combustion chambers, or even fuel injection. This new engine would take a conventional approach to generating power that with few changes could be adapted for passenger cars and trucks.

The first order of business, in Keinath's view, was to do away with the W-valve configuration and the combustion chamber–in–block design. With the freedom afforded him by virtue of the carte blanche mandate from Knudsen, Keinath was able to start with a clean sheet of paper. Displacement remained at 409ci. Virtually the only dimensions retained from the W-engine were the bore centers of 4.84in and the crankshaft-center-to-camshaft-center distance. These two dimensions have remained common to all Chevrolet big-block passenger car and truck V-8s.

Mention should be made here concerning the Mk (Mark) engine designations. This identification was first implemented, according to Keinath, by Duntov. Although the new engine taking shape on Keinath's drawing board had the same displacement as the W-configured 409ci V-8, Duntov called the new engine the Mk. By default, the W-engine series became the Mk I, and this set a precedent that has followed to this day.

The key to high output has always been the ability of an engine to breathe at high rpm. The Mk I 409 was constrained in this regard owing to its valve and port configuration. With the W-engine, the port arrangement was dictated by the pushrods. From the front to the back of the cylinder head, the valves ran intake-exhaust, exhaust-intake, intake-exhaust, exhaust-intake. For the new cylinder head, the valves were positioned intake-exhaust, intake-exhaust, and so on. This gave more latitude in the size and configuration of both the intake and exhaust ports.

According to Keinath, the intake ports were designed for smooth, uninterrupted flow with a minimum surface area–to–volume ratio. Numerous wooden models of different port configurations were made and flow-tested on an airflow bench in the carburetor flow room, since induction system flow benches had not yet been developed. The cylinder head configuration necessitated the design of two different length ports from the intake manifold plenum area.

"The shorter port," emphasized Keinath, "provided increased airflow around the inlet valve and also gave improved air-fuel mixing after being introduced into the cylinder, thereby yielding higher horsepower. Efforts were made to also improve the longer port, but we ran out of time for a complete development. Recently, a new generation of engineers has 'rediscovered' this relationship of port design to valve configuration, air-fuel charging, and [their] effect on obtaining higher horsepower."

Port configuration was also influenced by the intake and exhaust valve juxtaposition on the new cylinder head. First, rather than being placed parallel to each other, as was done with the small-block V-8, the valves were rotated several degrees within the combustion chamber, with the intake valve nearer the intake port and the exhaust valve nearer the exhaust port. Then, the intake valve was positioned 26 degrees from the vertical and the exhaust valve was tilted 17 degrees from the vertical, with the two having an included angle of 9 degrees in relation to each other in the cross-sectional view. Finally, the valves were tilted again, away from each other, along the camshaft axis—each valve 4 degrees, for an included angle in this plane of 8 degrees.

This splayed valve configuration looked curious, to say the least, and some clever individual coined the term *porcupine head* to describe it. Each valve, rocker arm, and pushrod operated within its own plane. Naturally, the camshaft and lifters were "flat"; the discrepancy of the compound angles of the pushrod was made up at the point where the pushrod and lifter made contact. Instead of broached slots being included in the cylinder head for the pushrod guides, cast-iron guides were designed and secured to the cylinder head. Subsequently, stamped metal guide plates were de-

The large readable instruments made it easy to keep tabs on the big-block Corvette's performance. For some today, low tech is still best. The four-speed manual transmission was standard in the Corvette, allowing the driver to take full advantage of the big-block's torque and horsepower.

The Mk IV intake manifold for standard passenger car use was a cast-iron design with oval ports. The high-performance intake manifold was a high-rise design with larger rectangular ports and was cast in aluminum.

The 425hp L78 came with a solid lifter camshaft, high-rise aluminum intake manifold, and Holley carburetor. The L78 option cost $292.70.

signed and secured to the cylinder head by each pair of intake and exhaust valve rocker arm studs. This approach provided excellent rocker arm stability and pushrod control. Keinath received a patent for this entire valve-train design.

The stamped steel rocker arms had a 1.65:1 ratio, compared with a 1.75:1 ratio for those on the W-engine, pivoting on 7/16in-diameter studs and secured by a rocker pivot ball and locknut made of sintered metal. The straight-sided valve covers were held in place by eight screws.

"One of the more extensive developments included the design, procurement, and testing of camshafts with various lifts, timing, valve overlap,

Next page
Chevrolet designed a custom showboat, Surfer I, to show off its new 396ci big-block Mk IV V-8, which was painted to match the colors in the boat. With open headers, the 396ci V-8 was more than a little loud. Surfer I was an entire rig, including boat, trailer, and El Camino, which was also powered by the new big-block V-8.

The 325hp version of the 396ci V-8, RPO L35, was the base big-block in 1965. It was offered only in Chevrolet's full-size cars that year.

The highest-rated 396ci big-block in 1965 was the 425hp L78 installed in the Corvette. One key to the engine's output was the exhaust manifolds, which employed individual runners and were so well designed that they were subsequently used on the L88 and ZL-1 427ci V-8s. Bolted to the engine is a Muncie four-speed manual transmission.

and valvetrain dynamics," Keinath remembered. "To appreciate this effort, we must remember that all camshafts were designed by hand, with no computers yet available. The camshafts were made without the use of computer-aided manufacturing. A minimum of twelve different camshaft configurations were designed, procured, and evaluated."

One of the pioneering efforts made by Keinath and his group was to determine the effect of valvetrain weight, stiffness, and harmonics (frequency) on the dynamics of the valvetrain system. "We procured many parts to reduce the mass of the valvetrain," Keinath recalled, "including shorter and lighter valve lifters, lighter pushrods, lighter valves, and thinner valve spring caps. The entire system was designed to run at a higher rpm in order to fully utilize the larger ports in the manifolds and cylinder heads for increased power. The big discovery was the fact that the lighter valvetrain components did not appreciably improve the valve performance without the necessity of also increasing the valvetrain stiffness. Again, new camshaft profiles, and ramps, had to be designed when we became aware of the effects of valvetrain natural frequency and angular acceleration upon total deflection and valve bounce. These developments were all made without the use of sophisticated equipment but by trial and error running actual engines on the dynamometer."

Perhaps the most visually prominent features on the engine were the exhaust manifolds. The cylinder head exhaust ports were designed virtually round, and the exhaust manifolds were essentially cast-iron headers matched to the exhaust ports. A great deal of flow testing was done to these manifolds, and they performed beautifully. Individual runners were grouped inline on the right and clustered in a diamond pattern on the left where they bolted to the steel tube head pipes, in order to clear chassis components. The length of each runner from the exhaust port to the 4in collector was 40in.

The bottom end of the cylinder block was structured much like the bottom end of the cylinder block on the

W-engine. Interestingly, the two-bolt main bearing design was also retained. A wide channel was provided to accommodate four-bolt main bearing caps. Chevrolet encountered few problems with the Z-11, or competition 409, however, and saw no need to go to four-bolt main bearing caps for the Mk II.

The 3.5in-stroke crankshaft had the same 2.5in-diameter main bearings and 2.2in-diameter rod bearings as the W-series 409. The crankshaft system had some newer features such as cross-drilled main journals, "thumbnail" grinds for improved oiling, and various bearing configurations for increased durability. The 409 connecting rods were beefed up and lengthened 0.125in. The pistons were necessarily new. The 12.5:1 aluminum pistons were forged—Chevrolet had always referred to such pistons as "impact extruded"—with a prominent pop-up section conforming to the combustion chamber to achieve the desired compression ratio.

The intake system included a dual-plane 180-degree high-rise aluminum intake manifold. Actually, three different induction systems were designed and evaluated. One included an acoustically tuned inlet system from the carburetor to the inlet valve, specifically designed for the Daytona race. It set up a harmonic pressure wave that reinforced the fuel-air mixture as it entered the cylinder at the inlet valve, thereby creating a partial supercharging effect. Atop the manifold sat a Holley four-barrel carburetor with 1 11/16in primary and secondary bores. The engine would incorporate the new cowl air intake system pioneered by Vince Piggins, eliminating high underhood air temperatures and boosting performance dramatically.

With the extensive prototype and manufacturing facilities at the Chevrolet Engineering Center, Keinath and his team members were able to get components for testing quickly. Parts for which the center did not have equipment, such as crankshafts and camshafts, were handled by local Detroit firms. Patterns for the Mk II were done by the Chevrolet foundry, and the prototype engines assembled at the Engineering Center. Because Keinath's team was small

and essentially clandestine, he was able to move fast and bypass the time-consuming review and procurement procedures that were a basic part of building production engines.

"We didn't have that many people working on it," he said. "It's just that everybody was so highly dedicated and I had picked various suppliers throughout the city that I had known through the years and worked with on the small-block, the four-cylinder, the six-cylinder, and other engines. I knew where to go to get things done, be it crankshafts, camshafts, valves, pushrods, or whatever. We had suppliers all over, but they were hand-picked with the procurement group. I would call the suppliers into my office and say, for example: 'I want you to make a camshaft for me. Can you have it by next Wednesday?' The same with valves, pistons, rings, and so on. A lot of this was done without drawings—just sketches. But everything was covered by paperwork, budgets, and work orders. All the long-lead items that required a lot of work, I started without drawings."

Keinath and his team were well into the Mk II engine development when NASCAR announced a change in maximum displacement to 427ci in November 1962. Keinath got a call from McPherson the day after the NASCAR announcement, saying to push the Mk II displacement to 427ci.

"The block stayed basically the same. All I had to do was open up the bottom end so I could put a larger crank in it. It then became the Mk IIS, because of the longer stroke," Keinath said.

The Mk IIS engines destined for Daytona were meticulously assembled, then tested at the center, crated, and shipped to to the track several days prior to the qualifying races.

The racers set to run the Mk IIS at Daytona were Junior Johnson, Johnny Rutherford, Bubba Farr, G. C. Spencer, and Rex White. Johnson won the first 100-mile qualifying race with an average speed more than 7mph over the record for that race. Rutherford won the second 100-mile qualifier, setting a record of 165.183mph for the average lap speed. These wins raised eyebrows all over Daytona, and soon the racing community was abuzz

about Chevrolet's new engine—the engine no one could seem to get a look at. The press was turned away at the garages where the cars were kept, questions were sidestepped with a shake of the head, and photos were not allowed—at first. The automotive press at Daytona began to refer to the engine as a mystery.

The most curious of the car companies represented at Daytona was Ford. The rules stated that only production engines could race in NASCAR events, and Ford teams became suspicious. It was here that things began to unravel for Chevrolet. Among the throngs at Daytona trying their best to look inconspicuous were Keinath, McPherson, and Rosenberger.

"When we won the qualifying races," Keinath remembered, "the top brass at GM phoned Knudsen and congratulated him. They didn't know the engine wasn't an old-fashioned 409. Ford went to NASCAR and said, 'This is an experimental engine. According to NASCAR rules, it has to be a production engine. Therefore, we want the Chevrolets all disqualified.' [NASCAR's] Bill France and all the NASCAR people got upset, obviously. Here they had these Chevys, the biggest drawing card they ever had at Daytona, the media had all this hype, and the people were coming to Daytona in droves. They couldn't disqualify Chevrolet. Public opinion would be, 'You're going to disqualify these cars because they're going to beat the Fords? What are you, Ford lovers?'"

NASCAR did the only thing it could do and enforced the rules. A hasty call was made to Knudsen about the dilemma. Knudsen weighed the alternatives and called Rosenberger in Daytona with his decision.

"I can remember when we took those engines down to Daytona," Rosenberger said. "We took eight, maybe ten engines. There was a rule that if you were going to run an engine

Next page
Even after more than a quarter of a century, the 1967 Camaro remains handsome. The Camaro Rally Sport SS396 with black-out grille, hood louvers, white paint stripe on the nose, and Red Line tires made a subdued and effective performance styling statement.

in the race, it had to be available for sale–and Ford exercised their option. After they saw that thing [our engine] run so fast and knew what it would do, they put the pressure on and said, 'We want to buy two of those engines.' When Bunkie called me down there and said we were going to do that because of the rule, I said: 'Bunkie, I'd rather take them out and dump them in the ocean than I would to give them to Ford, because we aren't far enough along with that engine in production. They'll have a whole year or two on us to look it over, and it isn't fair to us to do it.' He said: 'I know, but there's nothing I can do. The engine has gotten them all excited, and we have to live by the rule.'

"I even called Cole and told him what was on, and he said: 'I don't see any way out of the thing. We'll just have to let them go.' So we delivered two of them we had down there to Ford. The next day, one of the Firestone people I knew very well said: 'Well, we got an invitation to go over and see Ford's layout of your new engine. They laid it out down there for everybody to see.' What we should have done was not to take any spare engines down there, but they probably would have been able to rule against its [the new engine's] running."

It is possible the Firestone representative was ribbing Rosenberger. Keinath didn't remember Ford putting on a display of the engine and felt that instead, the engines were spirited back to Ford in Dearborn, where they could be inspected under controlled conditions.

"It seems to me Ford shipped them back to Dearborn," Keinath recalled. "They wouldn't tear them apart at Daytona. There would be no point to it."

Detailed news of this engine was leaked in the form of an article by Ray Brock that appeared in the May 1963 issue of *Hot Rod*. How this came about is a story in itself.

"After we had won the qualifying races, everybody started asking about the fast Chevys—where did they come from?" Keinath recalled, smiling. "I'll never forget this sight: Smokey Yunick had cyclone fence around his garage, and literally hundreds of racing enthusiasts were hanging on the fence trying to look in to see what the Chevys had.

"As I remember, the media pressure was so great, the race crews got to Vince Piggins and asked him if there was anything he could do to get the media off their backs. So Piggins talked it over with Rosy and Knudsen and said: 'Why don't we pick a magazine to interview Keinath and McPherson? Give them the pictures. By the time the article comes out, the race will be over and it will have satisfied the media craze.' Vince knew Ray Brock of *Hot Rod*, so we did an interview with Ray, but it was very secretive. We didn't even have it at our motel."

The engines did not do nearly as well in the Daytona 500. Three of the five Mystery Engine cars dropped out. The first five cars across the finish line were Fords. Still, questions persisted over this new engine.

At a GM press conference in Detroit the month following the races, President John Gordon and Chairman Frederic Donner were asked about this mysterious new engine, since the corporation supposedly was adhering to a no-racing policy. The two men were embarrassed to confess they knew nothing about it. Knudsen was called immediately thereafter and grilled concerning the matter.

The executive committee required a lot of explaining. Knudsen was called downtown, and Cole was probably in on this meeting also. Of course, by that time, Cole knew of the program and understood what the engineers at Chevrolet were really trying to do. Knudsen knew the technical superiority of the new engine and believed in it. He defended the Mk II program on the grounds that it would permit Chevrolet to build strong, performing street engines to compete with the large-displacement V-8s being created and planned by Ford and Chrysler. GM management in general and Cole, the group vice-president, in particular, had to agree with this view. The problem lay with

After the L78, the most powerful 396ci V-8 in 1965 was the L37, available only as part of the Z-16 option package on the Chevelle Malibu. The hydraulic lifter L37 developed 375hp running an 11:1 compression ratio. The four-speed close-ratio manual transmission was standard.

Chevrolet actively participating in racing when it had been strictly forbidden to do so. One can only imagine the conversations that took place on the fourteenth floor of the GM building in the aftermath of the Daytona 500 debacle. Undoubtedly, a few people suppressed smiles. No heads actually rolled, however, and that was good because Chevrolet had too good a team of engineers for anyone to be shown the door.

A new edict was issued in April 1963, and this one was strictly enforced. The dream of Chevrolet racing glory faded. Still, vast sums of money had been invested in the program. The unstated goal of the Mk II program, owing to its secrecy, was to provide a technical and manufacturing base for a new line of street engines to replace the W-series. Consequently, Mk II engine development continued. Chevrolet could not offer engines for racing, as it had at Daytona, but *testing* the engines was perfectly all right.

Prototype Mk II engines were built in a number of displacements. "We had 396ci, 409ci, and 427ci versions of the Mk II," Bill Howell recalled. "We did continuous development of the Mk II from the time it came off the drawing board in 1962 until we started development work on the Mk IV. I had Mk IIs running originally as 409s and 427s, and even a 396. I can't tell you exactly what year we quit, but it was [the] last part of 1963 or early 1964. We had them in full race versions over 500hp."

The Camaro interior went a long way in making the car immensely popular with the young and the young at heart. This SS396 is fitted with the optional Turbo Hydra-matic transmission.

The Mk III Engine Study

To many Chevrolet big-block enthusiasts who know that the Mystery Engine was referred to as the Mk IIS and the subsequent engine family starting with the 396ci V-8 was called the Mk IV, the question often arises: Was a Mk III developed?

During the summer of 1963, the Chevrolet engineers were looking at a different engine possibility having greater cylinder bore centers for a much larger displacement engine. But as Bill Howell related, the program was quickly abandoned.

"The Mk III never got off the drawing board," Howell remembered,

With valve covers removed, the staggered and splayed valves of the 396ci V-8 are visible. The cylinder heads show that Chevrolet had mastered thin-wall casting. Unlike those in the small-block V-8, the Mk IV big-block cylinder heads featured a machined valve cover surface. This engine is pictured with a Rochester Quadrajet carburetor.

"but the reason it was assigned a number was, Chevrolet was going to buy the Packard V-8 tooling when Packard went belly up. Chevrolet was going to buy the transfer equipment for tooling the machine line to build that engine and was going to redesign it, and as-signed the designation Mk III, but it didn't last long."

Evolution of the 396ci V-8

After the Mystery Engine tremors that had shaken the foundation of the GM building in Detroit had subsided, Chevrolet engineers in Warren, Michigan, got down to work putting the new big-block V-8 into production. The engineering program for this powerplant was larger than the one for the W-engine because it involved several different displacements, based on passenger car or truck applications.

A cornerstone of the W-engine program had been the use of a universal cylinder head regardless of passenger car or truck application. With the new Mark engine series, that concept was abandoned. Thus, more design, engineering, and development testing occurred with the new Mk IV engines.

On October 18, 1965, an SAE paper titled "Chevrolet Turbo-Jet Engine" was presented by Dick Keinath to the Detroit Section of the SAE. The authors of the paper were Keinath, Herbert G. Sood, and William J. Polkinghorne. In the introduction, the authors wrote:

"In the early 1960s, a change became apparent in the attitude of the majority of automotive buyers. An up-

swing in the national economy was increasing customer demand for larger, more luxurious, and better performing automobiles.

"Typical of this new trend was a shift in Chevrolet engine orders. In 1960, 47 percent of Chevrolet passenger car engines were V-8s. After 1961, demand for the V-8 engines increased sharply and it was determined that this trend toward larger engines would continue. This appraisal proved correct as V-8 sales have increased each year. In the 1965 model year they accounted for 67 percent of Chevrolet production.

"Concurrent with the increase in passenger car power options, a growing demand for heavy-duty trucks continues to be evident.

"In response to this growing demand in the automotive market, the Chevrolet Engineering Department began plans for a new series of larger displacement V-8 engines.

"This move was made even though the Turbo-Fire 409 cubic inch engine had been in production for only a year. The '409' had been tooled for relatively low volume and would not meet future needs.

"Approval for the new engine program included complete design freedom. In addition, the engine was to be adapted to modern, highly automated production methods.

"The result is a new line of V-8 engines available for Chevrolet cars in 396 and 427 cubic inch displacements, a 366 cubic inch heavy-duty truck engine and a 427 cubic inch heavy-duty marine engine.

"From the design standpoint, the most important characteristics of the new engines are superior breathing, increased combustion efficiency and improved durability.

"To achieve the objective of high volumetric efficiency without compromise, the design and development pro-

This was what 396ci of big-block V-8 looked like in 1967. The Tonawanda assembly plant affixed to the right valve cover a label proudly stating the engine's origin.

gram began with the establishment of the inlet port and exhaust port location and configurations.

"Once a cylinder head design was established that provided the optimum in breathing, all other components were designed around this basic functional area."

The tone of the introduction of this SAE paper was matter-of-fact; it gave the reader the impression that this engine was conceived strictly to meet Chevrolet Division's passenger car, truck, and marine requirements. No mention, of course, was made of the Daytona Mystery Engine–the Mk IIS. In truth, the engine *was* conceived to win in NASCAR but subsequently was engineered to meet the stated market requirements.

Why was 396ci chosen as the displacement for the first Mk IV introduced in 1965 and available in the Corvette, Chevelle, and full-size Chevrolet?

"The only reason that displacement fell out of the sky," Howell explained, "was because that was going to be the legal displacement for NASCAR. Our people, because they didn't have good communications with NASCAR, felt that that was going to be the engine size they were going to have to live with, so they did a bunch of design work around that displacement. Later on down the road, when they had to make a decision on a production engine, they decided to make it 396ci.

"The race engine work went on the back burner in 1963, when they pulled the rug out from under us in February at Daytona when they wouldn't let us go on with the current Mk II. So we went to one dynamometer cell for high-performance race engine development. We started phasing in street high-performance engine development. That would be any engine that ran rectangular port heads. I ran the development tests on that, and when they started making the oval port head production engine stuff, they assigned that to another test engineer and the two developments proceeded in parallel but entirely separate. There was some cross-fertilization, but not much.

"All the mechanical lifter high-performance street engines used the big rectangular ports, and I had all the mechanical lifter engine development. Plus, I had some stuff in odd cases where they put a hydraulic cam in a big-port engine like the Z-16 Chevelle. The Z-16 was the L78 mechanical lifter engine with a hydraulic cam in it. Everything else was the same."

The Mk IV Cylinder Head

The V-8 engine group worked closely with the Tonawanda Engine Plant in New York, configuring the sand cores to be used in casting the cylinder head. In the 1965 SAE paper, Dick Keinath, Herb Sood, and Bill Polkinghorne wrote:

"The new engine design reduces the number of cylinder head cores to three. The innovation of green sand molding of the combustion chamber and the combining of the intake and exhaust ports to a common perimeter core, were all made possible through a combined effort of engineering and foundry personnel.

"The reduction in the number of cores to produce the cylinder head substantially decreased production requirements for core equipment, dryers, and handling. In addition, the ability to make all the intake and exhaust port in one piece increased foundry accuracy considerably."

The valvetrain geometry of the Mk IV production V-8 remained virtually unchanged from that of the Mk IIS racing engine. The differences, briefly, were in the intake manifold and cylinder head porting, which was altered to optimize the Mk IV engine for street use; the cam timing and lift; and the deck height, which was taller at 10.2in, and camshaft, which was gear driven, for heavy-duty truck use.

The employment of established features of the Mk IIS in the Mk IV in no way diminished the full-fledged research, design, and development and durability testing that ensued. In this respect, the Mk IV was not different from any other new engine program at Chevrolet.

This SAE paper was also significant because it explained, in production terms, the design principles behind the concepts that had been used in the Mk IIS racing engine and were also employed in the Mk IV V-8 engine.

The paper revealed: "The angled position of the valves in the cylinder head and the modified wedge-shaped chamber allow a more direct flow of air-fuel mixture into the combustion chamber. The greater angle of the

Mk IV big-block V-8s, as far as the eye can see! The painted valve covers and standard exhaust manifolds of these newly assembled engines mean they are destined for standard passenger car use. Carburetors, air cleaners, and accessory-pulley drives will be installed later. This photo was taken in 1966.

Next page
The 1969 Chevelle 300 Deluxe two-door sedans ordered with the SS396 option were rare in number. Rarer still were those ordered with the L89 aluminum cylinder heads. Only six L78 and L89 examples were built that year.

inlet valve provides a more streamlined approach for the fuel charge and better utilization of the valve annulus at high engine speeds. The vertical position of the 409 necessitated a sharper turn [through] the ports. The new design results in more efficient cylinder charging.

"The plan view of the ports also shows a more direct flow path. The older Chevrolet engine has a circumference of 6.1 inches giving an area of 2.3 square inches. In contrast, the new cylinder head, with a reduced circumference of 5.7, gives an increased area of 2.5 square inches. This reduction of surface to area ratio through the port, in combination with the area increase, contributes appreciably to the volumetric efficiency improvement realized in this new design. The performance version has even larger ports..."

Regarding the exhaust ports, the authors had this to say:

"Exhaust port configuration has also been improved. The exhaust valve position made it possible to design a larger radius exhaust port with a more gradual directional change and an unrestricted cross-section through the passage length. In addition, the offsetting of the exhaust valve toward the exhaust side of the engine minimized the port length, thus reducing the amount of high temperature port area exposed to engine cooling."

Keinath, Sood, and Polkinghorne also wrote of the effort to ensure valve spring durability:

"The valve spring received careful attention during the design and development program. As development progressed, it was apparent that even though the stress of the pretest spring was in the 130,000 psi [pounds per square inch] range, spring durability was a problem. Therefore, it was decided to design a spring that would provide a solid height stress in the 130,000 psi range rather than a valve open load stress in this range.

"The loads required of the spring were the same as, or close to, the pretest even though the valve lift was more. This necessitated cylinder head changes to allow for a 1.88 inch valve spring space which was adequate for both present requirements and future. The major portion of this work was based on the high performance engine,

because this presented the extreme operating conditions.

"Further development showed a definite need for improved valve spring piloting. The cylinder head was revised to provide an outside diameter pilot to stabilize the bottom of the valve spring. At the spring cap area, a shoulder was designed into the cap to provide a pilot on the inside diameter of the valve spring damper. At this time a hardened steel washer was provided between the valve spring and the cylinder head to eliminate any possible wear problem due to spring rotation at high speeds."

The combustion chamber of the Turbo-Jet V-8 was closely patterned after that of the Mk IIS. The modified wedge chamber improved thermal efficiency over that of the W-engine by reducing the surface-to-volume ratio. Less piston area was exposed owing to the "bathtub"-shaped combustion chamber, and less heat was dissipated through the piston. Most of the combustion chamber was machined to further unshroud the intake and exhaust valves, maintain an accurate combustion ratio, and eliminate the foundry slab core operations.

As designed and developed for the standard passenger car and truck uses, the original combustion chamber proved adequate. For high-performance applications, power development tests showed that modifications needed to be made to the combustion chamber and exhaust ports. The changes included removing the protrusion near the spark plug and altering the area around the exhaust valve. It was hoped that the same core for the exhaust port could be used in trucks and cars, but this was a restriction in the high-performance big-block V-8. Engineers redesigned the area behind the exhaust valve around the valve guide in conjunction with opening up the adjoining exhaust port. The combustion chamber and exhaust port modifications boosted output by 20hp.

Such horsepower gains were the result of extensive power development in the dynamometer labs at the Chevrolet Engineering Center. Bill Howell was in charge of performance development of the Mk IV high-performance street engines. "Horsepower comes from airflow," he said. "The

more air you can pump through a given-displacement engine, the more power you can get, because you can always match it with fuel. Anything that controls airflow is subject to power development. It starts with the carburetor, the design of the intake manifold, design of the camshaft, the ports in the cylinder head, valve sizes–anything that affects airflow.

"We started this long before the Pontiac GTO, which brought big-block performance to the public. It kind of evolved with performance cars in the sixties, and we were in a good position because we had a good engine design with the Mk IV to do the Chevelles, Corvettes, and big-block Novas.

"Basically, the parameters came from the design group–Keinath's group. My job was to maximize the performance we could get in any particular area they wanted to concentrate on. I had a lot of flexibility in what I was able to test. Once we scheduled a test, GM has a book of roughly fifty different tests that are designed to test what you want to know. You look at the results, and from that we determined the degree of success–or failure. If something didn't work the way it was supposed to–and they seldom do–then your contribution as a test engineer might be to come up with another way to test it or a recommendation for improvement based on the test results. Ultimately, you reach the goals or exceed the goals the design group had in the first place. With the Mk IV, we consistently exceeded the goals for performance and, ultimately, for durability."

Rosy Rosenberger said, "I can remember after we had run one of those engines enough to know it put out about 100 more horsepower than any 348 or 409 we ever had on the dynamometer. I remember telling [Ed] Cole how good the new big-block engine was in production of power and torque, and he said: 'Yes, but we don't need it. You know, we've already got a good truck engine now.' I didn't have

Next page
The original owner of this car special-ordered Hugger Orange. Given the rarity of the body and engine combination, this is probably the only example in existence finished in this color.

The L78 396ci for 1969 was rated at 375hp. The L89 aluminum cylinder heads were available on the L71 427ci, which was optional in the Corvette in 1967 and 1968. They became an option on the L78 in Chevelles for 1969.

much of a retort for that. We did have an engine that was adequate for trucks. But, I did remark to him, 'Well, it won't put out any power [for racing], and you know if we're going to be out there exposed as we are, we can't put up with an engine that doesn't have power.'"

Mk IV Component Design

The intake manifold for the standard passenger car 396ci V-8 was cast iron. The high-performance intake manifold was very different. It was cast aluminum, had larger ports, and

had an enlarged plenum area beneath the carburetor.

"It was determined early in the program," the 1965 SAE paper stated, "that the additional manifold volume below the carburetor pad provided increased mid-range and high end power. Considerable effort was expended to revise the corners of the inlet manifold to provide even air distribution from cylinder to cylinder. The entire high performance induction system was evaluated for air handling capacity by running compression pressures throughout the speed range."

The cylinder block was made of high-chrome-content iron alloy, having a 4.094in bore and 3.76in stroke. Firewall thicknesses were beefed up from those on the 409ci V-8. On the Mk IV, the clamping surface of the crankshaft main bearing cap was widened by 2in.

Next page
It was once thought that a 283ci smallblock V-8 was a hot engine to put in a Nova. When Chevrolet introduced the Nova SS396, it lent new meaning to the term muscle car. The car pictured here was assembled at Willow Run, Michigan, on January 27, 1969.

This offered much more stability to the standard two-bolt main bearing cap and provided the space necessary for the four-bolt main bearing cap on high-performance engines. The bolt on the high-performance V-8s was made of 8640 steel alloy.

The Mk IV crankshaft was beefed up throughout. It was forged from SAE 1045 steel, and the high-performance cranks were Tufftrided after the main bearing journals were crossdrilled from the crankshaft feed hole

Previous page
No flashy graphics, bulging hood scoops, or spoilers drew attention to the Nova SS396. The car's unassuming appearance made it a real sleeper on the street.

to the rod bearing, to ensure 360-degree lubrication. The main bearing diameter was increased from 2.5in to 2.75in, the main bearing thrust area was increased from 2.92in to 3.96in, and the nose diameter was increased from 1.25in to 1.62in. The connecting rod bearing diameter remained at 2.2in.

The Mk IV connecting rods were stronger and heavier than those in the 409. The I-beam cross section of the new rods was greater. The standard rods were forged from SAE 1038 steel with 207-255 Brinnell hardness. The high-performance rods and caps were forged from 4340 steel with a Brinnell hardness of 269-321.

Three different pistons were developed for the new Mk IV–series engines: standard passenger car, high-performance, and truck. Both passenger car versions had pop-up portions to increase the compression ratio, with a compression height of 1.77in. The truck piston was flat and taller owing to the extra oil control ring, with a compression height of 2.17in. The deck height on the truck block was 10.4in.

During the early phase of power development on the high-performance engines, the ring lands on the 11:1 pistons were collapsing, seizing the rings. This happened because of the wide, unsupported slots underneath the bottom ring land. These were replaced by drilled holes giving the land more support. This "closed"-type piston required more piston-to-bore clearance to avoid scuffing, which in turn increased piston noise. Chevrolet solved the problem by putting a barrel taper on the piston skirt, just below the ring

Until the SS396, the largest V-8 you could order in the Nova was the 350ci small-block. The Nova SS396 was rarely seen in its day, having a mystique that commanded attention.

land, combined with a 0.0018in taper. This allowed the engineers to hold the piston-to-bore tolerance to 0.004in.

Chevrolet performed extensive development testing on the camshaft for the solid lifter engines. In initial tests, the big-block was fitted with a solid lifter camshaft having a 0.48in lift and a 1.74in installed height for the valve spring. The redline was 6000rpm. Using the only method available to study valve motion–high-speed motion pictures–Chevrolet saw the valve bouncing on closing and what it called nose lofting. The engineering laboratory then obtained a new piece of equipment, an optron tracer.

"Through the use of the optron tracer," the engineers wrote in the

The 396ci big-block V-8 was available in the full-size Chevrolet from 1965 through 1969. This Impala SS396 convertible is from 1968. Chevrolet

SAE paper, "valve train development was accelerated greatly. Camshaft design theories were modified to a great extent, and in conjunction with optron results on valve spring dynamics, the RPM range was extended above the 7000 RPM range."

Tests were so encouraging that a similar program was instituted for high-performance hydraulic camshaft big-block V-8s to give them performance levels previously associated only with mechanical lifter V-8s.

As the Tonawanda Engine Plant tooled up for production of the Mk IV V-8, Chevrolet was confident it had designed and developed an engine that could meet every requirement and expectation of the market.

Mk IV Big-block Introduction

Chevrolet did not hold back in applying the 396ci V-8 to its car line for 1965, although for this one year, the

new engine coexisted with two optional 409ci V-8s. Ads for the availability of the 396ci V-8 in the Impala didn't start appearing until the spring of 1965. The hydraulic cam L35 developed 325hp at 4800rpm and 410lb-ft of torque at 3200rpm. The solid lifter version developed 425hp at 6400rpm and 415lb-ft of torque at 4000rpm.

The same engine was available in the Corvette. This was the only year the 396ci V-8 was offered in the Corvette because the 427ci V-8 came along in 1966. Only 2,157 Corvettes were ordered with the 425hp L78 in 1965, and they are highly prized today.

In the Chevelle Super Sport (SS), the standard big-block V-8 was the L79, which developed 350hp at 5800rpm and 360lb-ft of torque at 3600rpm.

And then there was the Z-16 Chevelle Malibu SS396. This special Chevelle coupe was unique not only for its stronger convertible frame underneath and beefed-up suspension components, but for the L37 available only in this model as part of the Z-16 option. Fed by a Holley four-barrel carburetor, model number 3869933,

with 1.686in primaries and secondaries sitting atop an aluminum intake manifold, the L37 developed 375hp at 5600rpm and 420lb-ft of torque at 3600rpm, running an 11:1 compression ratio. The hydraulic camshaft had an intake duration, including ramps, of 342 degrees and an exhaust duration of 356 degrees, with 122 degrees of overlap. The AMA specifications sheet on the Z-16 did not legibly give the intake lift, but the exhaust lift was stated at .50in. The intake valve diameter was 2.18in, and the exhaust valve diameter was 1.72in.

Car Life tested a Z-16 Chevelle for the September 1965 issue. The editors were curiously unimpressed with the car, perhaps because so many other similar cars were available. The four-speed manual–equipped car with a 3.31 rear axle reached 60mph in 6.5 seconds, and covered the quarter-mile in 14.9 seconds doing 98mph.

The other hot performer in the 1965 Chevrolet line-up was the 425hp Corvette. *Road & Track* got its hands on a four-speed version with a 3.7 rear axle. Despite the limitations of narrow-profile bias-ply tires, the car reached 60mph in 5.7 seconds and shot through the quarter-mile timing lights in 14.1 seconds at 103mph. With an open exhaust system and slicks, times could have been dramatically improved. The engine had so much torque, the Corvette could accelerate from 50mph to 70mph in second gear in only 2.5 seconds.

Although the 396 vanished from the Corvette in 1966, it became a big-block mainstay in the Chevelle SS and Camaro SS, was a popular option in the full-size Chevrolet, and provided awesome punch to the Nova SS.

In 1966, the 396 was offered in the Chevelle in three states of tune: the 325hp L35, optional 360hp L60, and 375hp L78. The Chevelle SS396 was a frequently tested car in 1966. *Motor Trend* was one of the first to test the car for the February 1966 issue. With the optional L60 engine (only $105.35), four-speed manual transmission, and 3.31 rear axle, the editors only managed to achieve a 0–60 time of 7.9 seconds, with a quarter-mile time of 15.5 seconds doing 89mph.

Car Craft achieved better times with a similarly equipped car but running a 3.73 rear axle. This example covered the quarter-mile in 14.98 seconds and tripped the lights doing 97.82mph. Simply putting slicks on the car dropped the elapsed time (ET) to 13.66 seconds doing 103mph. The magazine also tested an L60 Chevelle whose owner ran the car with a 4.88 rear axle and tube headers. The ET dropped to 13.25 seconds with a trap speed of 107mph. Finally, the camshaft was swapped for a radical 396/427 solid lifter grind, and the car achieved a 12.43 ET doing 114.94mph. Indeed, the 396 Mk IV had potential—which was not surprising, considering its heritage.

The 325hp rating of the L35 remained unchanged through the sixties. The L34 was rated at 360hp in 1966 and at 350hp from 1967 through 1969. The most powerful of the 396s, the L78, was rated at 375hp from 1966 through 1969. In 1969, the L78 cost only $252.80 in the Chevelle SS and $316.00 in the Camaro SS and Nova SS. The exotic L89 aluminum cylinder heads were available on the L78 that year. The L78/L89 engine package cost $647.75.

Chevrolet unleashed the 396ci V-8 in the Camaro for 1968. *Car Life* tested an L35-equipped Camaro SS396 with the Turbo Hydra-matic transmission and a 3.07 rear axle–definitely not a high-performance setup. The car managed a quarter-mile ET of 15.48 seconds at 91.9mph.

The 396ci V-8 remained the largest big-block available in the Chevelle, Camaro, and Nova for the remainder of the sixties, although some dealers around the United States–like Nickey Chevrolet in Chicago, Baldwin/Motion on Long Island in New York, and Chevrolet's own COPO division–could see that a 427ci V-8 would find its way under the hood. The displacement numbers 3-9-6 took on a mystique of their own, one that endures to this day. Then, in 1970, Chevrolet did a curious thing.

The 402ci V-8

For 1970, Chevrolet decided to increase the bore of the 396ci V-8 from 4.094in to 4.126in. The stroke remained at 3.76in. The resulting displacement was 402ci. Chevrolet was relatively quiet about this change. Magazine editors and readers became aware of it only by carefully reading the 1970 engine specifications.

Chevrolet surmised, wisely, that to announce the Chevelle SS402, Camaro SS402, or Nova SS402 would be a mistake, so the displacement medallions on all Chevrolets with these engines remained unchanged. Few people were the wiser. The 396/402 was dropped from the full-size line of cars. In its place, one could order the 400ci small-block V-8 or the new 454ci big-block V-8.

One of the most handsome cars to come out of the muscle car era was the 1970 Chevelle SS. *Car Life* tested an example with the optional 350hp L34 and automatic transmission and 3.31 rear axle. Such a setup was not ideal for the stoplight grand prix, and the acceleration times proved it. The car reached 60mph in 8.1 seconds, and covered the quarter-mile in 15.5 seconds doing 90.42mph.

In 1970, the 402ci V-8s were still good, high-compression engines. In 1971, however, the compression ratio dropped from 10.25:1 to 8.5:1 for the L34, which was given the new RPO

LS3, and the L78 was dropped altogether. In conjunction with the lower compression ratio, the combustion chamber went from a closed to an open configuration. Gone was the familiar bathtub-shaped combustion chamber. In an effort to reduce emissions, Chevrolet all but eliminated the quench area around the spark plug and opposite the spark plug. Lab testing had found the quench areas of the cylinder head to be a source of unburned fuel. Eliminating these quench areas reduced exhaust emissions. It also unshrouded the valves and aided breathing, restoring some of the performance lost to the lowered compression ratio.

The 402ci V-8 was no longer available in the Nova SS. It was dropped from the Chevelle for 1971 but returned in 1972. Thus, in 1971, the LS3 was available only in the Camaro SS396. The engine was now rated at 300 gross horsepower (ghp).

Hot Rod tested a 1971 Camaro SS396 with the venerable Muncie four-speed manual transmission and 3.4 rear axle. Even with the engine detuned to meet emissions standards, the car was a good performer, covering the quarter-mile in 14.827 seconds doing 96.3mph.

The days of the LS3 were numbered. This was due in part to the availability of the 400ci small-block V-8 and 454ci big-block V-8. The LS3 was caught in the middle, and Chevrolet really had no clear-cut need for it. Its last production year was 1972, as it soldiered on in the Camaro SS396 and Chevelle SS. With the adoption of net horsepower (nhp) ratings and further detuning, it was now rated at 240hp. Still, hot rodders could get a good performance car for less than $5,000 and add a Holley carburetor, an aftermarket aluminum intake manifold, and a hotter cam, and they had a very entertaining set of wheels.

The 396/402 was in production for eight years. A great many examples of this engine are still out there, and they make excellent rebuilding projects. Once done, they are virtually bulletproof on the street and are great for bracket racing. Above all, they are Mk IVs, and they can proudly trace their roots directly to the engine that raced at the 1963 Daytona 500.

Chapter 4

The 427

The Big-Block Reaches Its Zenith

*We then decided there was a market for an
aluminum big-block racing engine, certainly in
Can-Am racing, and drag racing. Vince [Piggins],
more than anyone else, lobbied for an aluminum
version of the 427 block.*

–Bill Howell

To this day, few engines evoke as much admiration among Chevy enthusiasts as the 427ci big-block V-8—and with good reason.

The 427ci engine line launched in 1966 began an era of big-block high performance that began with the L72, culminated with the L88 in 1967, and ended with the ZL-1 in 1969. The 427 overshadowed the 396 as the performance big-block in the late sixties, finding a home in Corvettes, Impalas, and Caprices. Enterprising Chevrolet dealers and high-performance engine builders filled the midsize and compact void by asking the company to stuff 427s into Chevelles, Camaros, and even Novas. Chevrolet gladly complied with these requests through COPO options, with men like Don Yenko pioneering the way. If you wanted even more, there was Joel Rosen and the Baldwin/Motion Performance Phase I, II, and III earth shakers. Other dealers were more than happy to do the same. It was a glorious time.

Two of Chevrolet's premier production racing engines. In the foreground is the aluminum block ZL-1 of 1969, and in the background is its predecessor, the L88 of 1967. Both engines generated more than 500hp on the dyno with open headers.

The Impala SS427 was introduced as a distinct new model in 1967. Only 2,124 were built that year.

Although the 427ci big-block V-8 was conceived as part of the Mk IV program, which included a 427ci V-8 for both cars and trucks, it was introduced a year later than the 396ci Mk IV—in 1966. The primary differences between the truck and passenger car versions were a taller, 10.2in deck height to permit a four-ring piston and

a gear-driven camshaft, both found on the truck engine.

The 427 had a 4.251in bore and a 3.76in stroke. It had the same stroke as the 396ci V-8, thus permitting use of the same crankshaft and related parts. In fact, the only dimensional difference between the 396ci and 427ci V-8s was in the bore. This made durability testing more predictable and high-performance development easier and relatively inexpensive—initially. With the advent of the L88 and ZL-1, costs rose dramatically.

For 1966, Chevrolet introduced two 427ci V-8s: the 390hp L36 for Chevrolet's full-size passenger cars and the Corvette, and the 425hp L72 for the Corvette and Impala SS.

The L36 that year ran a 10.25:1 compression ratio. Pistons were cast aluminum. The connecting rods and crankshaft were forged steel. The engine block used two-bolt main bearing caps.

The intake valve diameter was a nominal 2.065in, and the exhaust valve diameter was 1.72in. The AMA specifications issued October 7, 1965, and revised March 25, 1966, gave an intake duration of 350 degrees and an exhaust duration of 352 degrees, including the ramps. The valve overlap was 118 degrees. The intake valve lift

The 427ci cylinder block differed from the 396ci cylinder block essentially in its larger, 4.251in-diameter bore. Truck versions and high-performance solid lifter automotive versions received four-bolt main bearing caps.

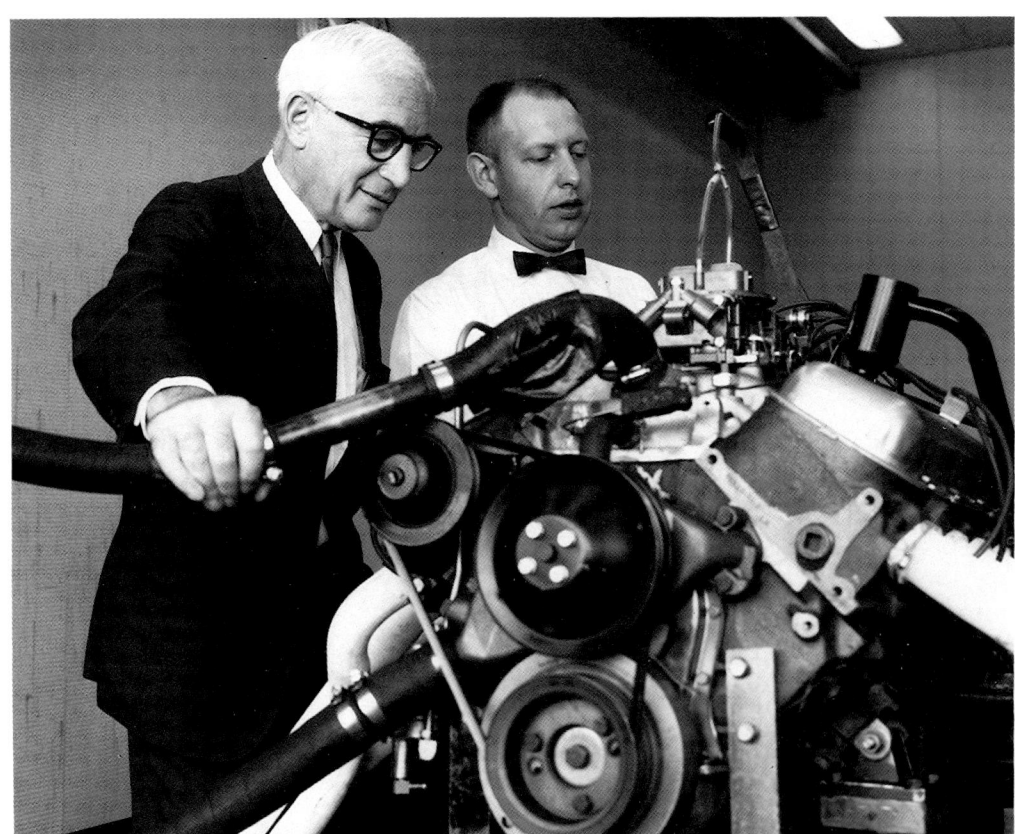

Zora Arkus-Duntov and Denny Davis in one of the dyno cells of the Chevrolet Engineering Center in May of 1966. The late sixties were the years of high-performance engine development for the Corvette. This 427ci big-block V-8 is being tested with tube-type exhaust headers. At this point, only the intake manifold was aluminum, but the days of the L88 and ZL-1 were not far off.

at zero lash was 0.4614in, and the exhaust valve lift at zero lash was 0.48in. The lifters were hydraulic.

The intake manifold was cast iron and was fitted with a Holley four-barrel carburetor, model number 3882835, with 1.562in-diameter primaries and secondaries. Atop the carburetor was a single-snorkel air cleaner. The L36 developed 390hp at 5200rpm and 460lb-ft of torque at 3600rpm.

The L72 was a serious street engine that saw considerable time at the strip. Pistons were forged, and the forged crankshaft journals were hardened using a low-temperature carbonitrided process. Four-bolt main bearing caps kept the bottom end together.

The L72 camshaft was mechanical. Its intake duration, including ramps, was 336 degrees, and its exhaust duration was the same. Its valve overlap was 108 degrees. Its intake and exhaust valve lifts at 0.024in lash were 0.5197in, and its exhaust valve lift at 0.028in lash was an identical 0.5197in. Interestingly, the AMA specifications for the L72 stated, "Values for 450hp are given with lash of .024 intake and .028 exhaust." That's why the 1966 L72 is sometimes referred to as a 425/450hp engine.

The L72 offered in the full-size Chevrolets came with a Holley four-barrel carburetor, part number 3885067. Holley carburetor part number 3886101 came on the L72 in the Corvette. Both carburetors had the same 1.686in primary and secondary throttle bores. The L72 in the Impala SS came with a dual-snorkel air cleaner. The L72 offered in the Corvette came with an open-element air cleaner. In 1966, the L72 was ordered in 5,258 Corvettes, and that was the only year this RPO was offered in the Corvette.

Chevrolet ran ads during 1966 telling enthusiasts of the division's newest big-block. "The big news isn't the gauges...it's what the gauges are connected to!" read one ad that ap-

Next page
Chevrolet's showroom brochure for the car read: "SS427/For the man who'd buy a sports car if it had this much room." Indeed, the convertible SS427 was the best of all possible worlds.

The L71 was sold in 1967, 1968, and 1969. It came with triple two-barrel carburetion and a solid lifter camshaft. It was the most potent Tri-Power big-block Chevrolet built, with a rating of 435hp. The engine pictured from 1969 is fitted with the AIR system to control emissions.

Vince Piggins joined Chevrolet in 1956 and immediately began to make his mark. He was the most visible promoter of performance Chevrolet had. His many successes included fresh air cowl induction, the Z-11, the Z-28, and the ZL-1 aluminum block 427ci V-8, to name just a few.

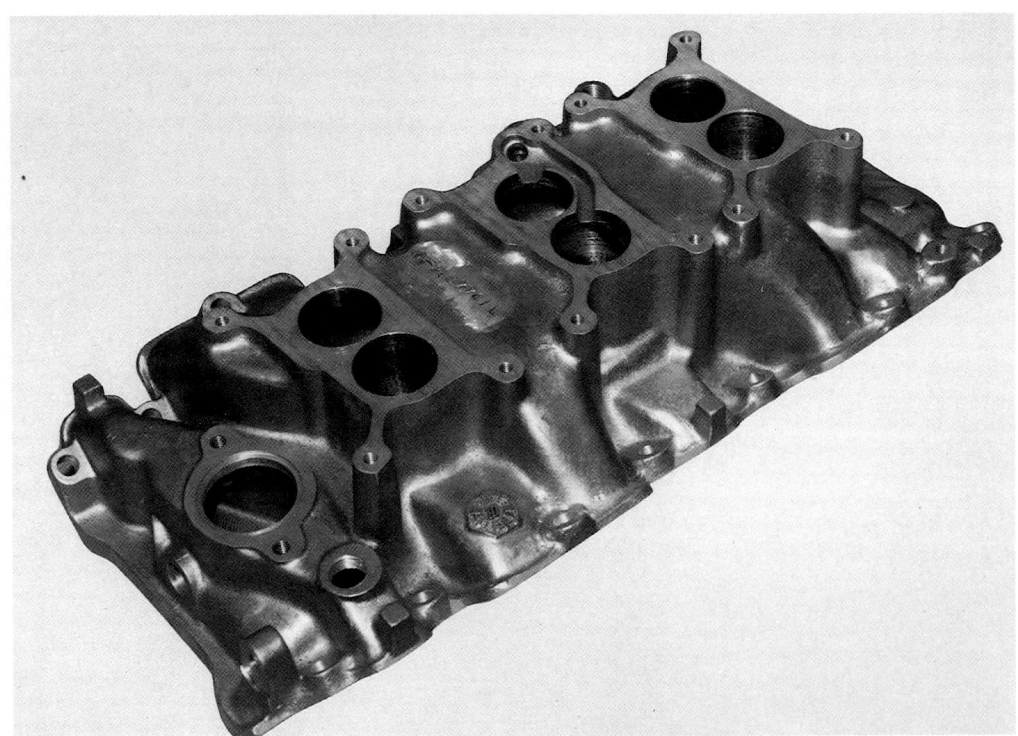

The Tri-Power intake manifold on the L71 was cast in aluminum by Winters Foundry; note the snowflake foundry mark. The four-barrel 427s offered nearly comparable performance with less complexity and fewer adjustment problems. Nevertheless, L71 Corvettes are coveted today and original manifolds command high prices.

peared in March 1966. The lead paragraph said: "The real news about Impala is the 427-cu-in. Turbo-Jet V-8 you can put on the other side of the firewall to make the needles quiver. The street version generates 390 hp and 415 lb-ft of torque on hydraulic lifters. A special purpose edition turns out 425 hp and the same amount of torque on solid (ah, what sounds!) lifters."

The more powerful 425hp version of these two engines was the L72. It was optional in the Impala SS for 1966, 1968, and 1969.

In 1967, the only 427ci V-8 available in the Impala was the L36, as part of the Impala SS427, a distinct new model. Since the same engine was optional in the Corvette, the L36 "lost"

Next page
Limited-slip differential was essential in getting all the torque the 427 could generate to the ground. It was an inexpensive option that permitted both rear tires to go up in smoke when the throttle was floored.

5hp in the Impala and was now rated at 385hp at 5200rpm and 460lb-ft of torque at 3400rpm, in deference to America's only sports car.

Car Life tested a 1967 Impala SS427 equipped with the new three-speed Turbo Hydra-matic transmission and 3.07:1 Positraction rear axle for its May issue that year. Despite the low numerical axle ratio, the editors found it difficult not to light up the rear tires during acceleration tests. With a curb weight of 3,835 pounds, the car reached 60mph in 8.4 seconds, and covered the quarter-mile in 15.75 seconds doing 86.5mph. Those wanting the best possible street performance would have chosen the optional four-speed transmission, RPO M20, with the optional 3.73:1 rear axle ratio.

The New Tri-Power 427ci V-8s

In the Corvettes for 1967, no less than four 427ci V-8s were available. The L72 was dropped, but three new 427s were offered, besides the 390hp L36.

Chevrolet introduced the L68, with three two-barrel carburetors,

rated at 400hp at 5400rpm and 460lb-ft of torque at 3600rpm. The L68 had the same hydraulic camshaft used in the L36. The triple two-barrel induction system marked the return of multiple carburetion to the big-block V-8. The intake manifold was cast aluminum by Winters Machine and Foundry in Canton, Ohio. The carburetors were Holley units. The center two-barrel–the primary–had 1.5in-diameter bores, with the model number 3902355. The forward and rear two-barrel carburetors–the secondaries–had 1.75in-diameter bores, with the model number 3902353. The L68 was a $305.50 option, and 2,101 Corvettes were ordered with it in 1967.

The L71 was, essentially, a Tri-Power L72. The intake and exhaust valve lifts were the same 0.5197in as in the previous year's L72. According to the AMA specifications, however, cam timing for the L71 was different. Taken at 0.024in of valve lash, the intake duration was 316 degrees. The exhaust duration, taken at 0.028in, was 302 degrees. The valve overlap was 80 degrees. The carburetors were

the same Holley units used on the L68. Running an 11:1 compression ratio, the L71 was rated at 435hp at 5800rpm and 460lb-ft of torque at 4000rpm. The L71 was a $437.10 option, and 3,754 Corvettes were ordered with it in 1967, so it outsold the L68.

A little-known option was available on the L71: Chevrolet introduced aluminum cylinder heads, RPO L89. Only sixteen buyers ordered the aluminum heads for their L71 'Vettes that year. The option cost $368.65. It also became available in the Chevelle SS396 in 1969 as part of the L78/L89 RPO.

The third new 427ci V-8 offered for 1967 was not listed in the Corvette brochure. That engine was the L88, an RPO that is revered among Corvette owners.

The L88

Among knowledgeable Corvette enthusiasts, *legendary* is not too strong a word to describe the L88. It was more than a racing engine; it was a vehicle, a concept made real by Zora Arkus-Duntov and his small band of engineers. But most of all, it was an RPO. It was offered in 1967, 1968, and 1969.

The L88 was an ambitious program to transform a production Corvette into a racing car that could take on the likes of everything from Cobras to Ferraris. In this, it succeeded. Performance it had in abundance, but, as owners and racers would tell you, it had weaknesses that sometimes snatched victory from their grasp–sometimes, but not always. And Chevrolet had an ongoing program of improvement to eliminate those weaknesses.

The L88 is legendary with reason. Stories like the following were not uncommon. Cliff Gottlob took delivery of his 1967 L88 Corvette Stingray directly at the St. Louis plant in August of that year. He was one of only twenty people who bought an L88 Corvette in 1967. Knowing the capabilities and rarity of the engine, he replaced it

The L89 cast-aluminum cylinder heads were an option on the L71 for its three years of production. Between 1967 and 1969, over 1,000 Corvettes were ordered with the L71-L89 combination.

Next page
The 427ci big-block as installed in the Impala SS427 was RPO L36 and was rated at 385ghp. This car was delivered with an incorrectly painted air cleaner.

78

The prime components of the finest big-block V-8 Chevrolet ever built–the ZL-1. They include the cast-aluminum cylinder block, cylinder heads, and intake manifold; a mechanical camshaft; an 850cfm Holley carburetor; 7/16in boron steel connecting rod bolts; 2.19in-diameter intake valves; and 1.88in-diameter exhaust valves. Note the machined plenum divider in the intake manifold and the round exhaust ports in the cylinder head.

with a Chevy small-block to take driving school courses, including Carroll Shelby's. He competed in regional events for two years, gaining experience and saving the L88 for bigger races in the future.

Late in 1969, he felt confident enough to set his sights on the 24

Hours of Daytona. As a matter of precaution, Gottlob replaced the only weak links he felt the engine had, installing stronger connecting rods and 11:1 pistons in place of the 12.5:1 pistons that came in the L88. He and co-driver Dave Dooley *drove* the L88 Corvette from their home state of Kansas to Daytona Beach, Florida, for the 1970 running of the 24 Hours of Daytona. At the driver's meeting prior to the race, Gottlob and Dooley were voted most likely to drop out during the first hour of the event.

The drivers and the car ran the entire race, sometimes hitting 186mph, and finished second in the Grand Touring class. They claimed their trophy before the cheering crowd while the drivers who did not finish

Next page
Two of the finest examples of Chevrolet big-block power in existence. The 1969 ZL-1 Corvette and the 1967 L88 Corvette are owned by Roger Judski, who operates Roger's Corvette Center in Maitland, Florida.

looked on in stunned disbelief. Then, the exultant Gottlob and Dooley got into the car and drove back to Kansas with the numbers still on the sides of the vehicle. This is the stuff of legends.

The L88 story begins, really, with the introduction of the 427ci V-8 in 1966. Behind the scenes at Chevrolet during the sixties, intense high-performance development work was being done on both the small-block and big-

The bottom end of the ZL-1 block was designed to withstand the most arduous competition use. The main firewalls were thicker than those on the iron block and featured four main bearing cap bolts with mounting studs for the windage tray. The tapped hole next to the number four main bearing is a provision for oil cooling components.

Installing the iron liners of the ZL-1 aluminum block involved a controlled process of heating the block, chilling the iron liners, carefully inserting and positioning the liners, and then allowing both the block and the liners to reach room temperature. The iron liners were machined to unshroud the huge intake valves. The curious drilled "bumps" above the first and third cylinders on this side of the block are the provisions for the two additional cylinder head bolts installed on each side from underneath.

block V-8s. Duntov's engine development group for the Corvette included Fred Frincke, Cal Wade, and Denny Davis. To be sure, others were working for these men, but this was the nucleus responsible for developing these engines in various forms, primarily for racing purposes.

A number of these high-performance big-block V-8s were truly exotic. These engines were strictly test beds and never saw production. They served to stretch the engineering capabilities of the engineers and show just what output could be achieved using various induction and valvetrain configurations. They included the chain-driven single overhead cam 427 running a 12.5:1 compression ratio, which developed 660hp at 6800rpm and 532lb-ft of torque at 4000rpm, and the pushrod 427 Hemi running an 11.3:1 compression ratio, which developed 628hp at 6400rpm and 552lb-ft of torque at 4400rpm.

Duntov wanted to see what could be achieved with the existing valvetrain configuration and single four-barrel induction on the 427, and raise it to a level that made it possible for the Corvette to be raced aggressively against the other high-performance cars of the day, foreign or domestic. He wanted to offer the serious Corvette racer an engine and car that would add prestige to the division–that would win races and stay together.

The L88 was a product of this period. A balance had to be struck between the exotic big-blocks testing the limits of the dynamometers at the Chevrolet Engineering Center and the street versions of the 427 coming off the assembly line at Tonawanda. In fact, this high-performance racing engine had to be a production engine, albeit limited, and available as an option in the Corvette.

Production drawings for the L88 were dated April 25, 1966. Revisions were made through the summer. Parts

Next page
The L88 Corvette made its debut in 1967 and was offered through 1969. For those three years, it waged war against everything from Cobras to Ferraris, was capable of exceeding 180mph on the Mulsanne straight at Le Mans, and survived the grueling 24 Hours of Daytona.

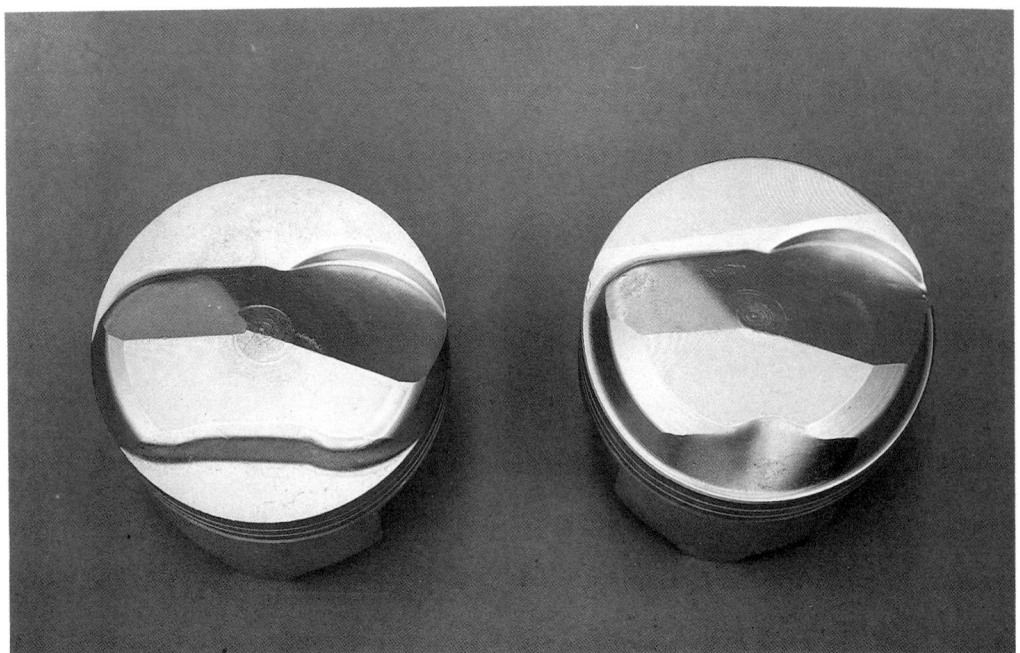

The piston on the left was used on the 1968 L88 engine. It was redesigned for the new open-chamber cylinder head used on the 1969 L88 and ZL-1, shown on the right.

The right cylinder head and valvetrain of the ZL-1. The Winters Foundry marks are clearly visible at the front and rear exhaust ports. Barely visible are the socket-head screws at the top of each branch on the exhaust manifold. These were removed when the AIR system was installed for the ZL-1 Corvettes and Camaros. Engines sold strictly for off-road use did not get the AIR system.

procurement began in the late fall and early winter. Chevrolet announced availability in the early months of 1967. This was too late for the engine to be included in the 1967 AMA specifications for the Corvette, issued on October 7, 1966. Apparently, Chevrolet did not publish revised specifications or separate AMA specifications for the 1967 L88 Corvette.

The L88 was based on the L71 427ci V-8 four-bolt engine block having the casting number 3904351. The forged crankshaft was unique to the L88; it was made from SAE 5140 steel alloy and Tufftrided. The connecting rods were also new and were shot-peened. The rod bolts were 3/8in, but these proved to be a key weak link among the reciprocating parts and were replaced in 1968 with 7/16in rod bolts. The forged aluminum pistons developed a 12.5:1 compression ratio.

The mechanical camshaft was more radically timed and had a higher lift than the L71's camshaft. The pushrods were a beefy 7/16in diameter with heat-treated hardened ends. The rocker arms were also unique to the L88 and were home to the new closed-chamber aluminum cylinder heads, which carried part number 3904387. The intake valves were 2.195in in diameter, and the exhaust valves were 1.84in in diameter.

The intake manifold was cast aluminum, with the plenum divider removed by machining to gain upper-rpm horsepower. The R3418 Holley 850-cubic-feet-per-minute (cfm) carburetor with 1.75in primary and secondary bores had to be specially calibrated so that the engine would idle, owing to the low vacuum generated by the camshaft.

A special air cleaner base was designed to clear this carburetor, with a screen around the carburetor intake and a foam surround that sealed against the opening of the fresh air hood as the hood was closed.

Next page
Above 150mph, aerodynamics can have as profound an effect on top speed as on horsepower. The sleek lines of the Corvette Stingray coupe were laid down by Larry Shinoda under the watchful eyes of Bill Mitchell, chief of styling.

At over $4,000 per copy, ownership of a ZL-1 was prohibitive for all but a few. Very limited production and hours of careful hand assembly under clean room condi-tions contributed to the unit's high cost. Consider what a ZL-1 engine still in its shipping crate would be worth today.

Despite the ZL-1 engine's full-fledged basis as a racing engine, it was designed to meet all emissions standards for 1969 so that it could be legally street driven. This fully as-sembled ZL-1 includes the AIR system with a belt-driven air pump. The air cleaner sig-nals that this engine is going into one of the two ZL-1 Corvettes built.

The cast-iron exhaust manifolds were the same as those on other high-performance 427s. Chevrolet, however, contracted with Bill Thomas, of Chee-tah fame, to produce headers for the L88, and these were available through the dealer parts department. The headers improved output significantly. Some sources stated they added as much as 100hp over the output of stock iron manifolds.

After the engines were assembled at Tonawanda, they were painted or-ange, including the aluminum cylinder heads and iron exhaust manifolds. Only the induction system was spared the spray gun.

One could not order just an L88 engine in the 1967 Corvette; the pow-erplant came with a list of mandatory options. Along with the L88 engine ($947.90), one must accept the J50 vacuum power booster with special proportioning valve ($42.15), J56 heavy-duty four-wheel disc brakes ($342.30), Muncie M22 heavy-duty four-speed manual transmission ($237.00), K66 transistorized ignition ($73.75), F41 suspension ($36.90), G81 Positraction axle ($42.15), and C48 heater-defroster delete option, for which one received a $97.85 credit.

Chevrolet took other steps to dis-courage the use of the L88 on the street as well as to reduce weight. You could not order a radio, power win-dows, air conditioning, or power steer-ing. Without question, this was a race car.

Another thing was missing from the L88 Corvette: the fan shroud. Testing of the L88 mule at the Milford Proving Grounds in Milford, Michigan, and the Desert Proving Grounds in Mesa, Arizona, determined that the engine cooled better at high speeds without the fan shroud, so it was elim-inated. Unknowing L88 buyers—there were a few—attempted to drive the car on the street, and it overheated at the lower street speeds A few insistent L88 owners had fan shrouds installed to permit street driving.

What kind of horsepower did the L88 develop? Chevrolet rated the en-gine at 430hp at 5200rpm, but total output on the dyno was around 560hp at 6400rpm, the engine's horsepower peak. This figure was achieved by Cliff Gottlob with his Daytona-winning

L88, number 21550. The engine had only 138 street miles and less than one racing season to its credit. Running with tube headers on 115-octane H & H racing fuel, the engine put out 437hp at 5200rpm and 560hp at 6200rpm; Gottlob did not want to take the engine to its redline. Unconfirmed reports gave drag strip quarter-mile ETs of 11 seconds at over 120mph.

For 1968, Chevrolet did issue separate AMA specifications–dated October 15, 1967–for the L88 Corvette. The engine was rated at 430hp at 4600rpm and 485lb-ft of torque at 4000rpm, running a 12.5:1 compression ratio. Chevrolet revised the connecting rods and rod bolts. The connecting rods were beefier and slightly heavier; the 1967 rods weighed 24.67 ounces, and the 1968 rods weighed 27.84 ounces. The rod bolts were now made of 10B-39 alloy boron steel, having a 220,000psi tensile strength, and were 7/16in in diameter. The crankshaft

had to be rebalanced to compensate for the increased reciprocating weight. The piston domes were redesigned; the sharp edges on the pop-up portion of the piston were smoothed. Minor changes were made in the oiling of the 1968 L88, with smaller, 1/8in pipe plugs installed.

Chevrolet came out with several camshafts available over the counter for the L88 and revised the camshaft as installed in the 1968 engine. Timing, based on top-of-ramp points, was as follows: the intake opened at 62 degrees and closed at 105 degrees, with 347 degrees of duration. The exhaust valve opened at 110 degrees, closed at 74 degrees, and had a duration of 364 degrees. The valve overlap was 136 degrees. The intake valve lift at zero lash was 0.5586in. The exhaust valve lift at zero lash was 0.58in.

Despite its racing intent, the 1968 L88 came with full emissions regalia. Gone was the simple road draft tube of

One quirk of the L88's production for 1967 at Tonawanda was painting the entire engine after assembly, including the aluminum cylinder heads. The engines were then shipped to the Corvette assembly plant in St. Louis. Only 20 L88 Corvettes were built in 1967. Note the absence of the fan shroud.

the 1967 engine. In its place was positive crankcase ventilation and a charcoal canister to trap evaporative emissions. Now the L88 was fitted with Chevrolet's Air Injection Reaction (AIR) system, which had a belt-driven air pump that fed air to the combustion pipe assemblies and fittings tapped into the exhaust manifolds to help reduce unburned hydrocarbons.

In terms of appearance, the L88 for 1968 had chrome valve covers and the aluminum cylinder heads were unpainted. Of course, this was the year of the new, Mako Shark–inspired

In the last year of passenger car production, the base 427ci big-block for 1969 was the LS1, rated at 335hp. The RPO number was a portent of the RPO numbers to come for the 454ci V-8 introduced for 1970.

The L36 was in production from 1966 through 1969. Its output remained at 390hp each year. Of all the 427ci V-8s built, the L36 was produced in the greatest numbers.

Corvette body design, and this required a new fresh air hood. The Chevrolet styling studio produced a design that was the most visually prominent of its day, and established a trend in aftermarket hood designs. It was available only with the L88 Corvette for 1968 and 1969 and on the 1969 ZL-1 Corvette.

For its February 1986 issue, *Road & Track* did a side-by-side comparison test of a 1968 L88 convertible and a 1986 L98 Corvette coupe with its 230hp 350ci tuned-port-injected small-block V-8. The test proved how far Corvette small-block V-8 technology had progressed in nearly twenty years. The L88 reached 60mph in 6.8 seconds, did 0–100mph in 13 seconds, and covered the quarter-mile in 14.1 seconds at 107mph. The L98 Corvette rocketed to 60mph in 5.8 seconds, ran 0–100mph in 16.2 seconds, and swept the quarter-mile in 14.3 seconds doing 96mph. The L88 topped out at a theoretical 154mph running a 3.36:1 rear axle; the editors did not actually take the car to its top speed, but extrapolated data from the first-, second-, and third-gear performances. The L98 Corvette achieved an actual 151mph in top gear.

Sales of the L88 quadrupled in 1968–to eighty cars. The engine option price remained unchanged at $947.90, but then one had to add those mandatory options.

Further changes were made to the L88 offered in 1969. That year, the L88 and ZL-1 were listed together on the AMA specifications for the 1969 Corvette, issued November 1, 1968. The L88 received open-chamber cylinder heads as part of a move by the division to improve combustion and lower emissions. The overall endeavor lowered compression to 12:1, but the unshrouded combustion chamber aided breathing. In addition, the cylinder head–the same one used on the ZL-1 V-8–had redesigned intake and exhaust ports. The exhaust ports themselves were round, and the exhaust valve diameter was increased to 1.88in.

Despite the L88's improved breathing ability, its rated horsepower wasn't changed. For some reason, the AMA specifications give the 430hp rating at 5200rpm, compared with

4600rpm the year before. Torque was 450lb-ft at 4400rpm, 35lb-ft more at 400rpm less than with the 1968 engine.

The price for the L88 engine option rose slightly for 1969, to $1,032.15. Incredibly, the base list price for the Corvette sport coupe was only $4,781.00. The convertible was even lower, at $4,438.00. For the first time, an automatic transmission was available with the L88. The M40 Turbo Hydra-matic transmission offered with all Corvette engines that year cost $221.80. Of the 116 L88 Corvettes sold in 1969, seventeen were ordered with this transmission, whereas the remaining cars came with the four-speed manual transmission.

Chevrolet never forgot the racers of big-block V-8s, despite the onslaught of emissions controls. The division continued to make L88 components available. The *1990 GM Performance Parts Catalog* still listed the L88 427ci partial engine assembly, part number 3970699, with the forged 1053 steel crankshaft, forged 4340 steel connecting rods and 7/16in boron steel bolts, and forged aluminum open-chamber pistons. The mechanical cam had a 0.54in intake lift and a 0.56in exhaust lift. You could also still order the L88 connecting rod, part number 3969804; boron steel connecting rod bolt, part number 3969864; and cam, part number 3925535.

The Mature 427

Perhaps the best-kept secret of the 1968 model year was the return of the L72 to the Impala option list. The brochure for the full-size Chevrolet didn't note its availability, so one had to read the enthusiast magazines to know that the meanest 427ci V-8 ever offered in the Impala was back. The L36-equipped Impala SS427, known as the Z24, was a paltry $358.10. The L72-equipped Impala SS427 was a $542.45 option.

All other 427s–the L36, L68, L88, and L71–were carried over for the 1968 model year.

Road & Track tested a 1968 Corvette convertible with the 435hp L71 fitted with the optional L89 aluminum cylinder heads. The editors had glowing things to say about this awesome automobile: "The aluminum-

The superior breathing ability and strength of the Mk IV big-block aided the design evolution of the L88. Performance gains were achieved from a new Holley carburetor, large passage high-rise aluminum intake manifold, and solid lifter camshaft specific to the L88. Tube headers were essential to achieve maximum horsepower. GM Powertrain

The L88 with its 12.5:1 compression ratio demanded racing fuel. Chevrolet alerted drivers to the engine's requirements with this warning label.

Previous page
Speculation abounds as to why only two 1969 ZL-1 Corvettes are known to have been built. It could be that the 1969 L88 Corvette offered comparable performance at one-fourth the option cost. Or the reason may lie within the files of Chevrolet's Central Office.

headed 427 engine costs nearly $400 more than its all-iron equivalent but is only 60 lb heavier than the 350.

"It is very flexible from 1000 rpm up and can actually be lugged smoothly from that speed in 4th gear. Its idle is another matter, being rough and noisy because of the big valve overlap and large displacement. There is a lot of tappet and fan noise under the hood

The ZL-1 Corvette received the same fresh air hood that first appeared on the 1968 L88 Corvette. The low stock hoodline of the 1968 Corvette necessitated a new fresh air hood to clear the high-rise intake manifold and double-pumper Holley carburetor.

The interior of the ZL-1 Corvette was no different than that of road-going Corvettes that year, except for the warning label on the center console. Although the ZL-1 could be ordered with automatic transmission, *the car was originally ordered with the four-speed manual transmission by George Heberling, St. Louis plant manager at the time.*

and a throaty bellow through its twin exhaust pipes that builds to a marvelous peak at its redline of 6500 rpm, which we used in the acceleration runs. As the performance figures show, there's simply no production car available today that can top its acceleration–and if we had used rear tires designed for dragging (the standard F70-15 tires on 8-in. rims spun freely getting off the line) we surely could have cut nearly a second off the quarter-mile time."

The L71/L89 Corvette reached 60mph in 6.1 seconds, and covered the quarter-mile in 14.3 seconds at 98mph. Clearly, tire technology was not up to the power of the engine.

Some changes were made to the 427ci big-block V-8 family in 1969. A new, bread-and-butter version was RPO LS1; its output was 335hp. Then came the familiar L36, L71, L72, and L88. The horsepower wars in Detroit were approaching a crescendo. Chevrolet announced a new 427 that was at the forefront of engine materials technology and power development–the ZL-1.

The ZL-1

In 1969, the L88 had to share the high-performance limelight with a new big-block: the all-aluminum ZL-1, the most exotic production Chevrolet big-block V-8 ever built. It was a logical step to take essentially the L88 and change the block from iron to aluminum. The modification was more involved than that, of course, for the new engine incorporated numerous changes and improvements to allow it to be used in more than just the Corvette for all-out racing. Can-Am competition was perhaps the hottest area of automotive racing in the late sixties. It was the cutting edge of racing technology, with advances involving chassis, engine, and body designs.

"The aluminum block stuff came about originally as a result of the Chaparral R & D [research and development] program when the Chaparral team decided that the small-block was no longer going to be viable against the McLarens and other competitors," said Bill Howell.

"They were also running a two-speed automatic transmission, and that transmission needed a lot of

torque. With only two gears, you need a broad engine power range.

"So in that program, they decided to go to the big-block in aluminum. They did from scratch an aluminum big-block with a built-in dry-sump system. It was an iron liner 427. They ran that as an exclusive with the Chaparral for one year. [Bruce] McLaren was running the cast-iron small-block when the Chaparral was running the aluminum big-block. McLaren said, 'We're going to see the people at Ford because we don't like being beaten by something we can't get.' That's when Vince Piggins got in the program. He instituted a meeting with McLaren to try to keep them from going to Ford. We didn't think Ford could deliver, but when you're in the romancing stage, anything is possible.

"We knew," Howell continued, "that the Roger Penskes and Bruce McLarens were successfully running Chevrolets and they could just as successfully run Fords or something else. We knew the deficiencies of the Chaparral program—at least Vince did—and I worked for Vince at the time, so I did, too. Part of the romance with McLaren was that we would get them the aluminum big-block. So we essentially duplicated what the Chaparral program had in 1967, made a run of those experimental castings and parts, and sold them to anyone who wanted to run the aluminum big-block in 1968. Of course, McLaren took it and dominated the field.

"We then decided there was a market for an aluminum big-block racing engine, certainly in Can-Am racing, and drag racing. Vince, more than anyone else, lobbied for an aluminum version of the 427 block. One of the smart things Vince always did was analyze something to find out whether we could compete with it in the first place, and if we couldn't, he wouldn't bother with it."

Funding to design and build a production racing 427ci aluminum V-8 was approved. It was natural that this assignment should fall to Zora Arkus-Duntov. Fred Frincke had been part of Duntov's small, select group of engineers working on high-performance engine development and had been involved in the Can-Am engine develop-

ment. Duntov felt confident giving the design task of the ZL-1 to him.

"Duntov had a lot to do with my working on the ZL-1," Frincke told this author. "I got pretty good at designing castings. I knew foundry problems, I understood patterns and pattern problems. Over the years, working with cylinder heads and manifolds so much, I got pretty good at designing that kind of stuff. I think that's why I was picked."

The ZL-1 cylinder block design began with a clean sheet of paper. The designers wanted to take into account aluminum's unique mechanical and thermal properties and also incorporate features desired by racers. Frincke laid it out along the dimensions of the L88 iron block and worked from there. The aluminum alloy chosen was 356 T-6.

The main bearing bulkheads were beefed up, and the forged SAE 5140 crankshaft was machined to get the

required clearance, but the main bearing journal length remained at 0.992in. A provision for dry-sump lubrication was added to the block. All high-performance Mk IV engines came with oil cooler provisions. Frincke added two bosses for cylinder head bolts at the deck surface of the cylinder block on each side so that the cylinder head would receive additional clamping force. The ZL-1 cylinder heads, also of 356 T-6 aluminum alloy, were considerably different from the L89 cylinder heads used on the L88 engine and optional on the L71.

Tests conducted at the Chevrolet Engineering Center proved that an open combustion chamber with a reduced squish area–the area between the piston and the cylinder head and outside the combustion chamber–produced lower emissions, with the added benefit of improved breathing. The volume for the new open combustion chamber was 118 cubic centimeters

The ZL-1 engine block can positively be identified by the two vertical ribs above the timing chain cover flange with the casting number in between. No other 427ci big- *block came this way. Although the ZL-1 engine block is unpainted, most engines were shipped from Tonawanda with painted engine blocks. GM Powertrain*

Whereas the ZL-1 Corvette was an RPO, the ZL-1 Camaro of 1969 was a COPO car. Their Spartan appearance gave no indication of what lurked under the hood. This example is one of only 59 originally built that year.

(cc), compared with 106.8cc for the closed design.

The intake ports remained at 3.84 square inches but were reconfigured to improve flow. Particular attention was paid to streamlining the valve guide areas. The exhaust ports were now round for a better match with tubular exhaust headers.

TRW engineered a new forged piston with a 12:1 compression ratio to conform to the open combustion cham-ber, and this was reinforced around the floating pin area and the skirt. Chevrolet assigned part number 3959105 to this piston. The connecting rods and bolts were the same ones used for the 1968 and 1969 L88s.

The intake valve diameter was 2.19in, and the exhaust valve diameter was 1.88in. The iron liners in the cylinder block were notched for intake valve clearance.

The camshaft was unique to the ZL-1. Although it shared similar timing with the 1969 L88 cam, the intake and exhaust lifts were greater for the ZL-1. Based on top-of-ramp points, the mechanical ZL-1 cam had an intake duration of 357 degrees, the exhaust duration was 364 degrees, and the valve overlap was 136 degrees–accord-ing to the AMA specifications for the ZL-1 Corvette that were issued November 1, 1968. The AMA specifications gave both intake and exhaust valve lifts at 0.58in, but these changed by the time the ZL-1 was in production. The finalized cam specifications were an intake valve lift of 0.56in and an exhaust valve lift of a whopping 0.6in. The Chevrolet part number for this camshaft was 3959180.

The induction package consisted of a high-rise aluminum intake manifold with the machined plenum divider; the casting number was 3933198. Atop the manifold was a Holley R4296-model 850cfm four-barrel carburetor. This unit had the same 1.75in-diameter primary and secondary bores as the 1968 L88 carburetor but featured

mechanical secondaries and was a double-pumper design. The Chevrolet part number was 3955205.

Winters Foundry was selected to cast the cylinder block, cylinder heads, and intake manifold. Its distinctive snowflake foundry mark is easily identifiable on its castings. The engine block was not machined by Winters, but was shipped to Tonawanda for cutting, shaping, and finishing.

Art Casper became involved with the Mk IV big-block from its inception and served in the capacity of industrial engineer overseeing the changes to the machining and assembly lines during changeover on an annual or midyear basis.

"I started at Tonawanda in March of 1964," Casper remembered. "At that time, we started installing the machinery to run the 1965 Mk IV 396/427 engine. All the Mk IV engines, except the ZL-1, ran down the same assembly line.

"We set up a special, in-house shop. We bought an Omni-mill, a programmable machine. By writing a computer program, it will select the proper tools and do progressive operations for you. We took the case (engine block) from the raw casting and ended up with a finished product.

"We heated the cylinder bores up with a blowtorch to make them expand, and packed the cast-iron sleeves in ice. Then we had only so much time to put the sleeves into the block before expansion rates started to take over.

"We had a special clean room set up. We had four or five employees, and their job was to assemble the ZL-1 in

an air-conditioned, clean environment; thereby, all the tolerances were maintained and all the engines were blueprinted before they left here. It took about 16 hours to build each engine. We weren't looking for a lot of volume because of the exorbitant cost.

"Each engine was serialized and then taken out to the test department where the engine was broken in for a 1-hour period. Then at that point it was taken down to our test lab, which was operated by our product engineering department, and it was run on a program down there. Each one of these engines had a performance chart associated with it. The advertised horsepower was 430 horse, but in reality, we never had an engine under 500hp. Every one that went out of here was between 500hp and 535hp on the dyno, running Sunoco 260.

"We built and shipped several ZL-1 engines to the Engineering Center. We have no idea what they went into, but I'm sure they went into executive cars for the most part. We had one running around here at Tonawanda in a white Caprice! My manager drove it."

Fred Frincke didn't remember any of these ZL-1 engines shipped to the Engineering Center being installed in cars as executive toys. To the best of his knowledge, they were used for further testing and development.

L88 and ZL-1 Development
Tom Langdon was the development engineer most closely involved with big-block high-performance development at the Engineering Center

The ZL-1 Camaro came with the same fresh air hood as offered on the 1969 Z-28. The clearance was sufficient so that a new hood did not have to be tooled up. Stock wheels and tires were dispensed with at the drag strip.

in the late sixties. He worked alongside Bill Howell and took over high-performance development duties when Howell was promoted. Langdon joined Chevrolet in June 1963 after graduating from Johns Hopkins University in Baltimore. The first few years he spent working as a dynamometer technician.

"When I first started work in the lab," Langdon recalled clearly, "it was a time when there was an occasional 409 running in the lab, but the majority of the involvement with the 409 was in truck applications. But you've got to remember that in 1963, the scene was changing rapidly from the W-engine toward the 396.

"Around 1966, I was promoted from technician to development engineer and was given a responsibility for following the high-performance development of the big-block engine, both in the street application, such as the L78 and the L72, and the off-road application, such as the L88 and ZL-1 and the aluminum block versions that were being developed for the Chaparral. I operated for about two years as a development engineer in the lab doing performance development work on those big-block engines, and then in 1968, I moved up into the design activity working for Fred Frincke in a simi-

The ZL-1 installed in Camaros came with restrictive cast-iron exhaust manifolds and stock dual-exhaust pipes and mufflers, effectively cutting the car's power nearly in half. Open-tube headers on the quarter-mile strip were the only way to go.

lar capacity over the big-block mechanical cam engines, both the street and high-performance racing type.

"The earliest development work that I did was on the 427 racing engine–the L88 during the 1968–69 time frame when we changed the cylinder head design from a closed chamber to an open chamber. The original purpose for that was emissions. The more open chamber was thought to be a more fully burning chamber with less quench area to reduce unburned hydrocarbons. There wasn't a major concern for hydrocarbons on racing engines; that wasn't the point. But we knew we were going to offer the big-

block engine in the full range of applications in trucks and passenger cars.

"Emission requirements were an emerging need. Our design activity at the time under Bill Polkinghorne had, upon recommendations from some of our emissions engineers, designed these cylinder heads with the chamber opened up to provide a cleaner burn with less quench area.

"When I say the cylinder heads," Langdon recalled, "instead of seeing reduced emissions, I saw them as potentially unshrouding the inlet and exhaust valves and increasing performance potential. When those cylinder heads were originally evaluated on the racing engines, they were evaluated with a compression ratio loss. We had been running at a 12:1 compression ratio, and when those heads were installed, we took a loss of 3/4 to 1 full ratio, and power actually went up slightly.

"We knew we had somewhat of an improvement on that cylinder head,

and we backed that up with some airflow evaluations that showed, yes, in fact, there was an improvement. As soon as we put the cylinder heads on and found we had some improvement in performance with the unshrouding of the valves, I got a bunch of heads and sent them out to all the different cylinder head porting shops in the Detroit area, a variety of well-known performance shops at that time. We had them do their best job porting and polishing the heads and had them brought back. We ran all the cylinder heads on the engine, picked the best ones, went back to the flow box, documented what they had to offer, and then tried to implement the design changes back into the cylinder head. All that culminated in the release of the open-chamber head for the 1969 L88.

"Secondly, along with the cylinder head design, I went back through a lot of camshaft work that had previously been done by Bill Howell and picked some similar camshafts that the engine had not previously responded to. I thought with the additional airflow capacity of the new heads, the engine might respond, and it did. The dynamics testing for durability on the high-speed optical displacement follower indicated it would be just as good from a durability standpoint. We were concerned about the durability of our valvetrain. That had been a persistent limiting factor on the durability of the engine when operating in a race application, so we were very cognizant of the limitations of the relatively heavy valvetrain. We found a camshaft which evolved into the release camshaft for the 1969 ZL-1.

"On the dynamometer, we did development work and durability testing. Our objective at those times was to complete a 24-hour high-speed durability test designed to simulate the 24 Hours of Daytona. A number of the engines we tested went to [the] DeLorenzo Corvette, which was a road racing Corvette. The engines were tested and run in and power checked, then shipped to DeLorenzo for installation in those vehicles.

"The ZL-1 Camaros were sold primarily for drag racing in a production environment. In those cars, we had exhaust manifolds—we didn't have headers—and we had a full exhaust system, which the ZL-1 was never intended to run with. They had to be streetable, but we were trying to do it in an economical way, and if we were to go to the time and expense of designing a specific exhaust system and a specific set of exhaust manifolds for that application, it would have been very time-consuming and expensive, and the racer's going to take it off anyway. It was expeditious for us to utilize the production environment to sell these vehicles, full well knowing that ninety-nine percent of them were going to run on the drag strip anyway.

"We did run some checks," Langdon said, "to see what the performance penalty was. A good ZL-1, when equipped with a standard set of aftermarket headers, would produce somewhere in excess of 500hp, maybe 525hp, without any attention to detail whatsoever. In other words, taking the engine, putting it on the dyno, putting on exhaust headers, and making it

run, you wound up with around 525hp, perhaps 600hp with some attention to detail to the cylinder heads, etcetera. We took one of those engines and ran it with a released exhaust system and got exactly half the power with Camaro exhaust manifolds, exhaust system, mufflers, and pipes. So you can see how sensitive the power was to the exhaust system when used with that ZL-1 racing camshaft. Power was cut to something like 275hp."

The ZL-1 Corvette and Camaro

Although the ZL-1 was an RPO in the 1969 Corvette, it was not an RPO in the Camaro. It could only be ordered in the Camaro as a COPO item.

Only two Corvettes are documented to have been built, not counting the pre-production car Zora Arkus-Duntov used at the press previews and any other test cars that might have been built. Fifty-nine Camaros were constructed with the ZL-1. More might have been built were it not for the engine's prohibitive cost. In the Corvette, the ZL-1 option was $4,718.35. By comparison, the L88 was ordered by 116 buyers in 1969, and it cost roughly one-fourth as much–$1,032.15, to be exact. Performance characteristics with the L88 and ZL-1 were virtually identical, the primary benefit of the ZL-1 being its lighter weight.

One 1969 ZL-1 Corvette, serial number 29219, was purchased by George Heberling, plant resident engineer at the St. Louis Corvette assembly plant. The car was painted Daytona Yellow with a black nose and fender stripe. Heberling street drove the car for approximately 2,000 miles before he was transferred to another GM division. The car remained at the plant, and the new resident engineer arranged for its sale. It passed through the hands of John Zagos, then Wayne Walker of Mechanicsville, Virginia, who fully restored it. Walker sold the ZL-1 in 1986 to Edward L. Mueller of Franklin Lakes, New Jersey.

In September 1988, the car was purchased by Craig Priest of Miami, Florida. Later that year, it was sold to Richard Lynn. The car was seized by the U.S. Marshals Service in May of 1990 and was placed at auction by the General Services Administration on

October 11, 1991, at Kennedy Space Center in Florida. Roger Judski, owner of Roger's Corvette Center in Maitland, Florida, successfully bid on the car, and it became part of his personal collection. This is the car featured in this book.

The other ZL-1 Corvette was originally purchased by Jack Cheskaty, who placed a special order for it at a Salt Lake City, Utah, Chevrolet dealership with a $500 deposit. When the car arrived at the dealership and Cheskaty flew in to take delivery of it, he noticed that it had just over 100 miles on it. The mileage on the car was a mystery, and he wondered if it had been put on a quarter-mile at a time. Nevertheless, he took delivery of the car and drove it back to his home in Denver. Cheskaty drag raced the car, as he had originally intended. The vehicle went through a series of owners during the seventies and eighties, then was purchased in the fall of 1987 for the Otis Chandler muscle car collection known as the Vintage Museum of Transportation and Wildlife in Oxnard, California. This car is featured in Randy Leffingwell's book *American Muscle*, published by Motorbooks International.

The ZL-1 production story went beyond these two installations, however. Fred Frincke received documentation from Tonawanda on the ZL-1 engine's total production that said 154 engines were built. It also stated 549 L88 engines were built.

In many respects, 1969 was a milestone for America. The United States achieved the age-old dream of rocketing to the moon and landing its astronauts there. In microcosm, Chevrolet built some of the fastest and most desirable cars available to buyers. The 427s were soon to disappear, to be replaced by the 454ci V-8. But the dyno rooms at the Chevrolet Engineering Center were testing the new-displacement Mk IV not so much for performance as for emissions, to be sure they met the more stringent government-mandated standards. The tall-deck 427ci V-8 for trucks continued in production and was still built at Tonawanda in 1992. In passenger cars, the 427ci V-8 was the zenith of big-block performance, and it went out shining.

Chapter 5

The 454

Long Live the Big-Block V-8

The LS7 was strictly for the Corvette and strictly for racing. It was an L88 with increased displacement. My memory tells me we never actually sold LS7s in a vehicle, but they did sell the engine and components.

–Tom Langdon

In 1970, Chevrolet introduced a new line of big-blocks displacing 454ci in its passenger cars and trucks. It was part of a GM decision to allow larger displacements in the 450ci range. Oldsmobile and Buick selected 455ci, Cadillac selected 472ci, and Chevrolet chose 454ci. With these new big-blocks, Chevrolet changed the RPO numbers. The 454 V-8s were the LS series.

Many enthusiasts recognize 1970 as the high-water mark of performance. Decompression took place beginning in 1971, and SAE net engine ratings were adopted across the board in 1972, lending the illusion of even more performance loss. Retarded ignition, softened camshaft profiles, and catalytic converters rang the death knell for the big-block V-8 in passenger cars. Consequently, 1970 was both a new beginning and the ending of the big-block era in Chevrolets. Fortunately, the big-block V-8 would soldier on in Chevrolet trucks and was discov-

What might have been: the ZR2. Engineer Scott Leon of the Desert Proving Grounds installed a modified TPI system on a marine 454ci V-8 in a 1989 Corvette convertible to see what it would do. Its performance rivaled that of the legendary L88 Corvette. Thomas Glatch

SS454 identification appeared on the side of the front fenders on the Chevelle SS. Without popping the hood, you would never know whether the car had the 390hp LS5 or the 450hp LS6.

ered by a new segment of buyers for use in marine applications. Technology during the eighties and nineties revived and improved it, and Chevrolet made a new push to interest the aftermarket buyer.

454ci V-8 General Specifications

"Shortly after the ZL-1 program," Tom Langdon explained, "the decision was made to increase the displacement on the engine to 454ci. Basically, all the packages that we had developed for the 396 and 427 were replicated in 454ci versions, which meant we had to go back and find out if the camshafts were applicable, and the compression ratio, and work out the durability and try to extend the power development from 427ci to 454ci displacement. Basically, the whole concept of the 427 was carried over to the 454. The cylinder heads were carried over, the compression ratio was carried over, and in fact, after some development work, the camshafts were carried over, both mechanical and hydraulic.

"The initial crankshafts that were supplied for the 454 were inferior in terms of strength, and we did have early failures. There was a redesign required where we widened the arms on the crankshaft and did some additional work on the torsional damper to gain satisfactory durability, and that set us back a little bit. Even prior to running durability tests, we had some crankshafts fail on the dynamometer during power development."

The 454ci V-8 received its displacement increase by means of a raise in the stroke of the 427 from 3.76in. to 4in. The nominal center-to-

The engine that never was: the Tri-Power 460hp 454ci V-8 of 1970. It was supposed to carry the L71 on to 454ci. The engine pictured appears to have aluminum cylinder heads. Multiple carburetion was dropped from the big-block V-8 in 1970, never to return.

The LS4 was introduced in 1970 in the full-size Chevrolet and was rated at 345ghp. It was not offered as an RPO again until 1973, when it became the sole 454ci big-block V-8 offered in Chevrolet cars. In its last year of passenger car production, 1976, it had a net rating of 225hp. This LS4 was photographed in 1973.

center length of 6.135in for the connecting rod was the same as in the 427, but the longer-throw crankshaft required relief notches at the bottom of the cylinder bores to clear the reciprocating connecting rods. The piston pin–to–crown height was reduced correspondingly. The longer-stroke crankshaft required additional counterweighting. Rather than alter the design of the engine block with a 4.251in-diameter bore, Chevrolet chose to balance the crankshaft using weights on the flywheel and front vibration damper.

Two low-rise intake manifolds for the 454 were designed and were distinctly different in the terms of the passages and ports. The 454ci V-8s used in standard passenger cars and trucks received a cast-iron, dual-plane intake manifold with individual spread bores, flanged for the Quadrajet four-barrel carburetor. The solid-lifter high-performance 454 V-8s got a dual-plane aluminum intake manifold that had larger passages, came with a plenum divider, and was flanged for the Holley spread bore carburetor.

The 1970 Big-block V-8 Lineup

Five distinct Turbo-Jet 454ci V-8s were originally scheduled for introduction in the 1970 model year. The *1970 Chevrolet Advertised Engine Ratings* for passenger cars, signed by Robert P. Bensinger and dated December 17, 1969, listed the LS4 in the Chevrolet; two versions of the LS5—one for the Chevelle and Monte Carlo and one for the Chevrolet and Corvette; the LS6 in the Chevelle and Camaro; and the LS7 in the Corvette and Chevelle.

Casualties occurred among these listings, however, and certain combinations never made it into production. Examining documents from the Chevrolet Division and the AMA reveals what might have been. Essentially, Chevrolet intended to carry over most of the 427ci high-performance V-8s in 454ci versions. Prohibitive insurance premiums and emissions controls loomed, however, and those, along with limited production, restricted or eliminated some of these V-8s.

The LS4

The Turbo-Jet 454ci V-8, RPO LS4, was the bread-and-butter big-block optional in the full-size Chevrolet. It was the lowest-rated of the 454s for 1970. Running a 10.25:1 compression ratio, it was rated at 345hp at 4400rpm and 500lb-ft of torque at 3000rpm.

The cylinder block, cylinder heads, and intake manifold were cast iron. The pistons were cast aluminum. The connecting rods, as always with Chevrolet V-8 engines, were forged steel. The crankshaft in the LS4 was also forged steel.

The valvetrain featured hydraulic lifters. According to the AMA specifications, timing–based on top-of-ramp points–included an intake duration of 280 degrees, an exhaust duration of 318 degrees, and a valve overlap of 91 degrees. The intake valve diameter was a nominal 2.065in, and the exhaust valve diameter was a nominal 1.72in. The intake valve lift at zero lash was 0.3983in, and the exhaust valve lift at zero lash was 0.43in.

The four-barrel carburetor was a Rochester unit, model number 7040200, with 1.38in primaries and 2.25in secondaries. The air cleaner was a single-snorkel design.

The LS4 was a veritable bargain, optionwise, costing only an additional $133.35.

The LS5

The LS5 was identical to the LS4 in all respects, except for the camshaft and rated output. Of the two LS5 V-8 versions produced, the one available in the Chevelle SS454 and Monte Carlo SS454 was rated at 360hp at 4400rpm and 500lb-ft of torque at 3200rpm. The LS5 available in the Corvette and full-size Chevrolet was rated at 390hp at 4800rpm and 500lb-ft of torque at 3400rpm.

The 360hp LS5 used a hydraulic camshaft. The AMA specifications gave timing, based on top-of-ramp points, with an intake duration of 350 degrees, an exhaust duration of 352 degrees, and a valve overlap of 118 degrees. The intake valve lift at zero lash was 0.4614in. The exhaust valve lift was 0.48in. This engine used the same carburetor as the LS4.

The 390hp LS5 was the top big-block you could order in your full-size Chevrolet or Corvette. It was identical to the 360hp LS5 in all respects except

for the rated output at a higher given rpm. Since the compression ratio and camshaft timing were the same for the 360hp and 390hp versions, the actual output difference between the two may really occur on paper only. The 390hp

LS5 used the same carburetor and air cleaner as the 345hp LS4 and 360hp LS5.

Road & Track tested a 1970 Corvette with the LS5 390hp 454ci big-block and an automatic transmis-

In 1970, Chevrolet introduced the Monte Carlo, its entry into the personal luxury car market. The long-hood, short-deck design proved popular with buyers.

The intake manifold designed for the 450hp LS6 was cast in aluminum and flanged for the Holley spread bore four-barrel carburetor.

The 1970 Monte Carlo came standard with a 350ci small-block V-8. The top optional powerplant was the 360hp 454ci LS5. The Monte Carlo SS454 was a rare sight in its day. A plate on the rocker panel was the only means of identifying the car.

sion. It was no rocket with a 3.08:1 rear axle, but this particular car wasn't meant to be, having many luxury options. The big-block 'Vette reached 60mph in 7 seconds and covered the quarter-mile in 15 seconds doing 93mph. Its top speed was 144mph.

Of the 454 LS5 Corvette, the editors wrote: "It is by far the most tractable big-engine Corvette unit we've tried; it idles fairly smoothly at 600 rpm with the automatic transmission in drive, but from outside the car there's still that monster rumble to let any and all know this is a big one."

The LS5 option in the 1970 Corvette cost $289.65. That year, 4,473 Corvettes were ordered with this big-block V-8.

The LS6

Things really began to heat up with the LS6. This 450hp big-block was scheduled for both the Chevelle SS and Camaro SS, but it was dropped from the Camaro line before production was authorized.

The AMA specifications issued for the 1970 Camaro on February 26, 1970, listed both the 375hp 402ci L78 (mistakenly entered on page 3 as an LS6–clearly a typo) and the 450hp 454ci LS6. The cover sheet of these specifications had this handwritten note: "LS6–454 cu in Engine Canceled [per] ECR 28389. Available as COPO Only."

Thus, the LS6 found a home only in the Chevelle SS454 in 1970, at least in terms of mass production, and this was the hottest Chevelle you could buy that year. According to the AMA specifications that were issued for the 1970 Chevelle on October 15, 1969, the LS6 was rated at 450hp at 5600rpm and 500lb-ft of torque at 3600rpm running an 11.25:1 compression ratio.

The cylinder block and cylinder heads were cast iron. The intake manifold was the low-rise cast-aluminum unit specifically designed for this engine. The closed-chamber cylinder heads featured larger-diameter, 2.19in intake valves and 1.88in exhaust valves. The pistons were forged aluminum.

The solid lifter camshaft was designed to really make the LS6 breathe. The AMA specifications gave, at top-of-ramp points, an intake duration of 316 degrees, an exhaust duration of 302 degrees, and a valve overlap of 80 degrees. The intake and exhaust valve

lifts at zero lash were 0.5197in. This cam gave the LS6 a glorious idle at 750rpm and an unmistakable sound that turned heads as the car accelerated from the stoplights.

The carburetor for this pavement pounder, of course, was a Holley with 1.69in-diameter primary and secondary throttle bores. The carburetor for Chevelles equipped with a four-speed manual transmission was model number 3967477, and Chevelles built with an automatic transmission got model number 3969898.

The LS6 was Chevrolet's most serious big-block in its most serious muscle car. *Car and Driver* tested the 1970 Chevelle SS454 for the February 1970 issue. Running a 3.7 rear end and a Turbo Hydra-matic transmission, the car reached 60mph in 5.4 seconds and 100mph in 13 seconds, and covered the quarter-mile in 13.82 seconds doing 103.8mph. It was fully up to the task of taking on 428 Ford Mustang CJs, 455 Buick Skylark GSs, 440 Plymouth 'Cuda Six-Packs, and even Dodge Hemi Chargers.

The base list price for the Chevelle was $2,809.00. Amazingly, the LS6 option was only $263.30, but you first had to order the Super Sport package, which cost $445.55. You did not want to go without power steering in this car, which cost $105.35. Not having bucket seats in a Chevelle SS was unthinkable, so you shelled out an additional $121.15. The limited-slip differential was $42.15 well spent. If you really needed the Turbo Hydra-matic transmission, it cost $290.40. Cruising in a car like the Chevelle SS454 without an AM/FM stereo radio was unimaginable, so you anted up the $133.80. Throw in a few amenities, and you were looking at nearly a $4,800.00 bottom line. That was a lot of money when you considered that a base Corvette convertible with a 300hp 350ci small-block V-8 and four-speed manual transmission—all standard equipment—sold for $4,849.00.

The LS7

Of all the 454ci V-8s, the LS7 remains an enigma. It carried the mantle of the L88 to 454ci, but a number of issues that are still unclear cut this engine's availability short. The first official document describing the LS7 was *1970 Chevrolet Advertised Engine Ratings–Passenger Cars*, dated December 17, 1969, and signed by Robert P. Bensinger. It listed the Turbo-Jet 454, RPO LS7, for use in Chevelles and Corvettes. With an 11.25:1 compression ratio, it was rated at 460hp at 5600rpm and 490lb-ft of torque at 3600rpm.

Clearly, the LS7 was set for production at this point. It had been designed, tested and emissions certified for the 1970 model year. The 11.25:1 compression ratio was the maximum Chevrolet could allow on the street with the octane rating of the gasoline available at the pump.

When the AMA specifications were issued in February 1970 for the Corvette and the Chevelle, the listings included the LS7 for the Corvette but not the Chevelle.

It is illustrative to compare the LS5 and LS7 initially offered in the 1970 Corvette. The LS7 piston was forged and weighed 29.12 ounces, whereas the cast LS5 piston weighed 26.8 ounces. The LS7 piston was slightly shorter than that used in the LS5 and had zero offset. The top land clearances for both pistons were identical at 0.0306in–0.0394in, but the top skirt clearance was 0.0058in–0.0066in for the LS7 piston and 0.002in–0.0028in for the LS5 piston. The material and configuration of the

piston rings were the same for both engines, but the compression rings in the LS7 had a width of 0.062in–0.0625in and a gap of 0.015in–0.025in.

Whereas the LS5 cylinder head was cast iron, the LS7 cylinder head was cast aluminum and featured the open-chamber design introduced on the ZL-1.

The closed-chamber cylinder heads of the LS6 featured a 108cc combustion chamber, 2.19in-diameter intake valves, and 1.88in exhaust valves. The closed-chamber head is identified by its bathtub-shaped combustion chamber. The part number of this casting is 3919840.

The exhaust side of the high-performance LS6 cylinder head. The splayed valve configuration is clearly visible in this view.

The small spark plug was adopted in 1970, replacing the larger plug also shown.

The connecting rods, as in all Chevy V-8 engines, were forged. The LS7 connecting rods were slightly heavier than the LS5's, at 29.44 ounces. The bearing clearance limits of 0.0014in–0.0034in differed from those on the LS5 connecting rod.

The LS7 crankshaft had slightly smaller main bearing journal diameters than the LS5's. The number one main bearing diameter was 2.7492in. Main bearings numbers two, three, and four were 2.7498in in diameter. The number five main bearing was 2.75in in diameter.

The LS7 camshaft was mechanical, and the solid lifters operated with a 0.02in clearance. The timing and lift of the camshaft were entirely different from those on the LS5 hydraulic cam, and even the LS6 solid lifter cam. The intake duration was 347 degrees, the exhaust duration was 359 degrees, and the overlap was a whopping 135 degrees. Lifts were 0.5197in for the intake and 0.5498in for the exhaust. The nominal intake valve diameter was 2.19in, and the nominal exhaust valve diameter was 1.88in.

Tom Langdon feels the camshaft specifications given in the AMA specifications for the LS7 are inaccurate. According to his personal notes, gross lift for intake was .584in and exhaust lift was .626in. His net figures give .56in lift intake and .600in lift for exhaust.

The AMA specifications for the LS7 list a Holley 780cfm carburetor, model number 3967481, with 1.686in primary and secondary bores, but Langdon disputes this—and he should know. Langdon says the LS7 ran with an 850cfm Holley having 1.75in primary and secondary bores. The intake manifold was that used on the ZL-1.

The AMA specifications for the Corvette stated that neither air conditioning nor power steering was available, which made it clear that this engine was designed for serious racing purposes. Nevertheless, the unit was certified with complete emissions control hardware, which at this point involved the AIR system to reduce emissions.

"The LS7 was strictly for the Corvette and strictly for racing," Tom Langdon stated. "It was an L88 with increased displacement. It had an iron block, aluminum cylinder head, and the ZL-1 camshaft, and the undivided intake manifold. It was a way to get racing components into the vehicle and out to the customer. My memory tells me we never actually sold LS7s in

a vehicle, but they did sell the engine and components."

As it had with the ZL-1, Chevrolet built an LS7 Corvette, undoubtedly the test vehicle. This car was the subject of a road test and article for *Sports Car Graphic*. The test driver was Paul Van Valkenburgh, who had worked at Chevrolet. Predictably, the car's performance was breathtaking. Unfortunately, the LS7 Corvette program never went through, and this prototype was destroyed, in keeping with the edict of the Environmental Protection Agency. It is a shame that an exemption can't be provided for such vehicles so that they might be kept for their historic value. It would be a tantalizing prospect to have the LS7 Corvette on display at the National Corvette Museum in Bowling Green, Kentucky.

The LT2

Perhaps the rarest 454ci V-8 Chevrolet ever built was the little-known LT2. Having an aluminum cylinder block and cylinder heads, it was a lineal descendant of the 427ci ZL-1. With a proverbial damn-the-torpedoes attitude, the performance enthusiasts among the Chevrolet engine group of engineers went ahead with a project to build an aluminum 454ci V-8. The likelihood of its being approved for production was not ensured in light

The most powerful 454ci V-8 offered in full-size Chevrolets and Corvettes for 1970 was the 390hp LS5. Its gross torque was 500lb-ft at 3400rpm. Its compression ratio was 10.25:1. A 360hp version was available in the Chevelle and Monte Carlo that year. The LS5 was last offered in 1972.

of pending emissions regulations, but it nevertheless was built and displayed at the press preview for 1970.

Engineer Fred Frincke can vouch for the LT2's existence. "We were starting to develop a 454ci ZL-1 called the LT2," Frincke remembered. "All we did was put a 454 crank in the engine and shorten up the piston. Only a

The 1970 Chevelle SS454 equipped with the 450hp LS6 big-block was a fine example of the muscle car genre. The original owner of this car chose not to order the hood and trunk stripes or the cowl induction hood.

handful of LT2s were built, and they were all experimental."

Changes for the Seventies

A number of key changes were announced in 1971, and they had a direct impact on performance. The first was lower compression ratios across the board, as a means of coping with low-lead gasoline and eventually unleaded gasoline. Lead contained antiknock and lubricating qualities, but it would have to be removed to cope with the forthcoming emissions requirements. Tom Langdon recalled the edict issued by Ed Cole concerning this:

"I can dramatically remember the announcement: 'You guys are going to get the lead out'–and that was virtually an overnight edict. There were

The LS6 option was offered in the Chevelle in 1970 and 1971. In 1971, the engine dropped from 450hp to 425hp when its compression ratio was lowered to 9:1. It still had monstrous torque. This car was one of the rare 1970 SS454 convertibles built.

enough senior engineers who had been around long enough and had experience with other types of unleaded fuel. They fully comprehended what a major impact that would have on the industry. Basically, we didn't know

The 454 HO sustains the high-output big-block legacy formerly carried by the LS6 aftermarket V-8. This engine comes with an 8.75:1 compression ratio, four-bolt main bearing caps, a forged 1053 steel crankshaft, a 0.51in-lift hydraulic marine profile camshaft, and an LS6 high-rise aluminum intake manifold. High Performance Communications

The 502ci short-block assembly was designed with racers in mind. It has a larger, 4.47in bore with an identical, 4in stroke. It serves as an excellent basis for engine builders to choose their own cylinder heads and camshaft. It is used in offshore power-boats, competition tractors, and, of course, serious quarter-mile contenders. High Performance Communications

where we were going to get enough nickel to make the valve seats that were required. The only known productive way of coping with unleaded fuel and still retain[ing] satisfactory valve seat durability was to install valve seat inserts which were high in nickel content.

"We didn't know where we could buy enough nickel to make enough inserts to service our engines. So, there was a mad rush on to develop new technology in production to cope with unleaded fuel and known seat recession. We knew we had a standard 200-hour dynamometer full-power test, and you could run that on leaded fuel and only see 0.025in or 0.03in valve seat recession with leaded fuel. But with the edict of unleaded fuel being given to us for 1971, we ran that same test, and the cylinder heads were gone in 25 hours. So we knew something had to be done overnight.

"That led to the development of the induction hardened valve seat," Langdon explained, "which virtually all iron-headed engines have today with the exception of special heavy-duty trucks, which have valve seat inserts. An electric inductor coil comes down in close proximity to the valve seat and heats it cherry red and then is quenched. Once you've bought the tooling and allowed for the time in the line, the cost of doing a valve seat is extremely low and totally satisfactory for all passenger car applications."

The next announcement was the adoption of net horsepower ratings for engines. These were a more realistic reflection of the actual output of engines as installed in cars. Making the change had a dunning effect on the cars' performance image based on advertised ratings, however, and lent the impression of a precipitous fall in performance. It was a perception that became fact over the next several years.

Nevertheless, big-block fans had good news to cheer about. The LS6 returned in the Chevelle SS454, and its availability was announced in the Corvette. The LS6 was also listed in the AMA specifications issued in September 1970 for the 1971 Monte Carlo, but this option was apparently dropped prior to the car's introduction.

The compression ratio for the LS5 available in the Chevrolet, Chevelle,

Monte Carlo, and Corvette was lowered to 8.5. The gross horsepower rating was 365 at 4800rpm, and the engine gave 465lb-ft of torque at 3200rpm. The net ratings were 285hp at 4000rpm and 390lb-ft of torque at 3200rpm. The camshaft timing remained unchanged.

The specifications for the LS6 available in the Corvette and Chevelle for 1971 were identical. The compression ratio was lowered to 9:1. The engine was rated at 425hp at 5600rpm and 475lb-ft of torque at 4000rpm. The AMA specifications gave net ratings of 325hp at 5600rpm and 390lb-ft of torque at 3600rpm.

The Corvette LS6 cylinder heads were cast aluminum with an open-combustion-chamber configuration having a volume of 119.09cc. The intake valve diameter was 2.19in, and the exhaust valve diameter was 1.88in. The camshaft was mechanical, with a tappet clearance for the intake at 0.024in and for the exhaust at 0.028in. Based on top-of-ramp points, the intake duration was 316 degrees, the exhaust duration was 302 degrees, and the valve overlap was 80 degrees. The intake and exhaust valve lifts at zero lash were 0.5197in. In short, the camshaft was carried over from 1970.

The Holley carburetor was also carried over from the previous year. The part numbers were new, however. The Holley unit used on manual transmission cars was part number 3986195, and the automatic transmission—equipped LS6 cars got part number 3986196.

Despite the lower compression ratio, the LS6 of 1971 was every bit the engine the LS6 of 1970 was. The aluminum cylinder heads were an added bonus that year; cast-iron cylinder heads were used on the 1970 and 1971 LS6 in Chevelles.

Production figures for the LS6 Chevelle SS454 are not readily available. Those for the LS6 Corvette are known, however: 188 were ordered in 1971, at a cost of $1,221. These two cars were really the swan song for big-block high performance, and smart buyers placed their orders and held onto the cars once they took delivery.

The situation for the 454ci big-block V-8 in the Chevrolet line of cars declined rapidly after 1971. The high-performance 454s were gone by 1972. The only big-block available in the Chevrolet line was the LS5. It was rated at 270hp at 4000rpm and 390lb-ft of torque at 3200rpm. Its compression ratio was 8.5:1. The camshaft timing and lift were carried over from 1971. As an indication of California's tougher emissions regulations, the LS5 was not available in that state.

In 1973, the LS4 was introduced to replace the LS5. The compression ratio was now 8.25:1. The forged crankshaft of the LS5 was gone; in its place was a nodular iron crankshaft. The camshaft timing was also softened. The intake duration was now 346 degrees, and the exhaust duration was 348 degrees, but the overlap remained at 118 degrees. The intake valve and exhaust valve lifts were reduced to 0.44in. The LS4 was rated at 245hp at 4000rpm and 375lb-ft of torque at 2800rpm. In the Corvette, the LS4 was rated at 275hp. The LS4 was designed to meet California's emissions laws, so sales of big-block Corvettes totaled 4,412 in 1973, up from 3,913 the year before.

The collector car hobby had not yet taken off, so many performance enthusiasts missed the opportunity to buy one of the most collectible cars today, the 1974 454ci Corvette. That was the last year the big-block was offered in the Corvette. The LS4 option cost only $250, and 3,494 buyers wisely chose it. Specifications remained unchanged from those in 1973, but the ratings were now 270hp at 4400rpm and 380lb-ft of torque at 2800rpm.

In the 1974 Chevrolet, Monte Carlo, and Chevelle, the LS4 was rated at 235hp at 4000rpm and 360lb-ft of torque at 2800rpm. What kind of performance did the emissions-era big-block offer? *Chevy Action* magazine tested an LS4-equipped Monte Carlo with the optional 3.42:1 rear axle. The car reached 60mph in 7.9 seconds, and covered the quarter-mile in 15.4 seconds doing 88mph.

Compare that to two big-block tests reported previously: A 1970 Corvette (390hp 454ci LS5 and an automatic transmission) reached 60mph in 7 seconds, ran the quarter-mile in 15 seconds doing 93mph, and posted a top speed of 144mph. A 1970 Chevelle SS454 (LS6 engine, 3.7 rear end, and Turbo Hydra-matic transmission) reached 60mph in 5.4 seconds, hit 100mph in 13 seconds, and ran the quarter-mile in 13.82 seconds doing 103.8mph.

The days of the 454ci big-block V-8 in passenger cars were numbered. The decision was made that 1975 would be

The four-speed manual transmission of the Chevelle SS came with a Hurst shifter.

This was the shifter to have in the sixties and the early seventies.

The LS6 made the Chevelle a serious contender in NHRA class racing and a formidable opponent on the street. Prohibitive insurance premiums and increasingly stringent emissions requirements slowly killed the engine.

the last year the engine would be offered in the Chevelle and Monte Carlo, and 1976 would be the last year in the full-size Chevrolet. In 1975, the compression ratio was dropped slightly to 8.15:1. That year, the LS4 was rated at 215hp at 4000rpm and 350lb-ft of torque at 2400rpm. With the 1976 model year, the big-block era in passenger cars came to a close.

Engineering Doldrums

A number of circumstances had taken their toll on the 454 big-block, and they made for depressing automo-

bile buying during the seventies. Emissions regulations and the push to unleaded gasoline forced Chevrolet to shift its engineering resources from performance development to emissions control. The 454ci big-block V-8 was dropped from the Chevelle, the Corvette, the Monte Carlo, and finally the Chevrolet itself. All the while, horsepower continued to drop and prices continued to rise. What was particularly distressing was that no light appeared to be at the end of the tunnel; emissions levels were scheduled to tighten increasingly through the seventies.

"It was no longer fun to come to work," Keinath remembered soberly. "It was a depressing time."

The whole thrust during the sixties had been in the area of improving the performance of the big-block. Many of the engineers at Chevrolet

had been involved in one way or another with some of the most exciting high-performance engine projects in the big-block's history. These were not emotionless individuals who cared little if they worked on a radical new high-performance mechanical camshaft or a cam profile to reduce emissions. They had passion for their work, and it depressed them to see the big-block slowly robbed of its superb, abundant power and then watch it vanish from Chevrolet's line of cars.

The enthusiast magazines tried valiantly to put the best face on the performance malaise, but they had to admit that times were bad. The 454ci big-block continued in trucks, along with the 366ci and 427ci big-block V-8s. Chevrolet never stopped building and selling its high-performance engine assemblies, partial engine assemblies (short-blocks), and high-perfor-

mance parts. A huge aftermarket, thankfully, still existed, and Chevrolet kept the production lines going to fill its needs.

"Chevrolet built this tremendous image of performance almost exclusively in the seventies when there was nothing going on with production cars," Bill Howell stated. "The performance image went off the street and onto drag racing and circle track. Chevrolet captured that market by having economical-to-buy and readily available parts. Also, during the sixties and seventies, we perfected backdoor racing policies to where we would maximize Chevrolet's image, even though the corporation wouldn't advertise the [racing] success.

"During this time period," Howell continued, "we recognized that grassroots racing was our salvation as a performance image. We started preserving our good high-performance parts from the sixties. In February 1963, the corporation cracked down on racing by Chevrolet and Pontiac. Pontiac eventually cut everything from its product line that had to do with performance. They quit making forged crankshafts, forged connecting rods, forged pistons—the good parts—and in four years they were nowhere.

"When Chevrolet pulled its horns back in, they said: 'Well, we better keep the forged crankshafts because we need them for trucks. We'll keep the premium forged connecting

The 1970 Chevrolet Caprice with the 390hp LS5 truly was a gentleman's or gentlewoman's express. The LS4 345hp 454ci V-8 was the other optional big-block available. The 454ci big-block was last offered in full-sized Chevrolets in 1976.

rods—they cost us fifty cents more but...' There were a lot of people at Chevrolet who were latent racers, and every time they could save a good part from the hangman, they did it. These were all production parts. You went into your Chevy dealer and bought them. We always kept them in the parts book, and people could always go to a dealership and buy them. The car magazines picked up on this. That's

Although the big 454 Caprice was not a contender on the quarter-mile strip in stock trim, tube headers, a 4.1 rear end, and some dyno tuning made it come alive.

where everyone else got behind, because it was going on under everyone's nose. It was right out in the open. You could buy all these parts from Chevrolet, and nobody else was putting two and two together and realizing what it was doing for the image."

A few alterations were made to the 454ci big-block during the seventies,

but fundamental changes took place in the eighties in terms of technology and basic engine design that revitalized the big-block, making possible new products for the nineties.

Throttle Body Injection

Emissions standards were not as stringent for trucks as for cars, and carburetors remained the means of air-fuel metering until the late eighties. Catalytic converters appeared on GM cars in 1975, but they were not installed on GM trucks until much later. Eventually, emissions standards did

catch up with trucks, and so did the technology to control truck emissions.

Research and development of throttle body injection (TBI) took place at the Emission Control System Project Center at the GM Proving Grounds in Milford, Michigan. Work was begun in the late seventies on a new means of low-pressure fuel delivery that was controlled electronically but was less complex and less expensive than the electronic fuel injection (EFI) developed earlier.

EFI was a high-pressure system operating at between 39psi and 79psi,

The LS5 as installed in the Caprice received the chrome dress-up valve covers but not the air cleaner. Despite the car's size, the engine compartment is filled.

requiring an expensive, precise, high-pressure fuel pump and an in-tank low-pressure boost pump. It was the goal of engineers at the Emission Control System Project Center to design an alternative to this expensive means of fuel delivery. Lauren L. Bowler, who worked at the center, wrote an SAE paper titled "Throttle Body Fuel Injection (TBI)–An Integrated Control System," which was presented in February 1980 at the SAE Congress and Exposition at Cobo Hall in Detroit.

In the paper, Bowler outlined the primary components of the TBI system. They are the throttle body unit itself and the electronic control module (ECM), otherwise known as the black box. Different models of TBI systems were planned for a variety of GM powerplants, each of them using variants of the five main components of the TBI unit. These components are (1) the fuel injector, (2) throttle position sensors, (3) the idle air control (IAC) valve assembly, (4) the fuel meter body assembly, and (5) the fuel meter cover assembly. The low-pressure fuel injectors were developed by the GM Diesel Equipment Division, which was consolidated with Rochester Products Division in 1981, with an eye on less expensive manufacturing procedures compared with those for the high-pressure fuel injectors. Rochester Products Division handled the throttle body itself.

The ECM was initially developed by Santa Barbara Operations, of GM's Delco Electronics, and manufactured at Delco's Milwaukee facility. This first-generation ECM included an 8-bit microprocessor with a sampling rate of 500,000 steps per second.

The microprocessor consisted of a GM Custom Microcomputer (GMCM) chip set incorporating large-scale integrated (LSI) circuits. These, in turn, included the microprocessing unit (MPU), power control unit (PCU), and engine control unit (ECU) and an 8-channel analog-to-digital converter of sensor signals for manifold absolute pressure (MAP), throttle position, coolant temperature, and barometric pressure. Finally, memory chips included an 8-kilobyte (K) read-only memory (ROM), a 256-word random-accessory memory (RAM), and a 1K programmable read-only memory (PROM).

Bowler summed up the benefits of TBI in the conclusion of his SAE paper this way:

"The beneficial features of General [Motors'] TBI have made this new sys-

113

The big-block Corvette remained in production until 1974. The rarest and most powerful 454ci big-block offered was the LS6 of 1971 with aluminum cylinder heads, of which only 188 were built. This 1972 model was available with the LS5. Chevrolet

tem an active contender for future engine control applications. These features include hardware simplicity, reduced evaporative emissions, excellent hot fuel handling characteristics, a single metering circuit to calibrate per throttle bore, elimination of ignition off dieseling (run on), full fuel range scheduling including cold start, alti-

tude compensation (with EGR [exhaust gas recirculation] compensation), and the flexibility to expand to closed loop with an exhaust sensor."

The GM TBI system made its first appearance on the 1980 Cadillac Eldorado and Seville, in keeping with corporate precedent to introduce the latest technological developments on its premier car line. The other GM divisions quickly followed, and TBI applications spread to trucks as well as cars during the eighties. TBI was first installed in trucks on the 2.5-liter L4 engine in 1985, and later that year was added to the 2.8-liter V-6 in the S/T

trucks and to the 4.3-liter V-6 in the M-van. In 1987, TBI application expanded to include light-duty trucks of up to 10,000 pounds GVW.

The carburetor disappeared from the 454ci big-block, replaced by TBI. The application of TBI in trucks and tuned port injection (TPI) in Chevrolet cars offered the technology base for some interesting projects to emerge from Chevrolet and GM Powertrain.

The ZR2: 'Big Doggie'

On the wall of Scott Leon's office at the Desert Proving Grounds is a plaque that reads, "If you can't run

with the big dogs, stay on the porch." It is a saying pertinent to sled dog racers in Alaska, where only the biggest, strongest, and toughest dogs can see the grueling races to the finish. Leon adopted the phrase to a project he had been wanting to do ever since the big-block V-8 was dropped from the Corvette after 1974. It involved installing a 454ci big-block V-8 in a late-model Corvette.

Leon started working at the proving grounds in the summer of 1973. His first task, interestingly, concerned cooling tests of the big-block Corvette. It wasn't until the eighties, with the adoption of TPI on the small-block V-

8, that the germ of the idea began to grow.

"I was running hot fuel tests on the small-block fuel-injected Corvettes when the performance started coming back," Leon stated. "It was interesting the performance gains to be had getting computers on board. I was interested from that standpoint of performance improvements brought on by fuel injection in the small-block and thought it would be neat if we did something similar to the big-block.

"The first fuel-injected big-block we built was in a pickup truck, easily modified, because it already had a Mark engine in it. The question was,

The last pre-bumper Corvette was the 1972 model. In 1973, the Corvette received a color-keyed 5mph front bumper. In 1974, it also got the federally mandated 5mph rear bumper. Chevrolet

'How do I fuel inject a big-block, and what would be the best platform for it?' So, the truck was a natural. We started with an aftermarket tunnel ram manifold, built a plenum that was big enough to straddle the tunnel ram, and put an L98 throttle body on the front. We put Buick Grand National fuel injectors on it, which flow forty percent more fuel than L98 injectors.

115

The 454ci big-block had been absent from the Corvette for 15 years until Scott Leon at the Desert Proving Grounds shoehorned one into a roadster just to see if it would fit. With the support of Chief Engineer Jim Minneker of Corvette Powertrain, the ZR2 became a reality. Thomas Glatch

Since a 454 is roughly thirty percent larger than a 350ci small-block, I figured if we powered this thing up with a Corvette ECM, it may run rich when you first start it up, it may run rich at wide-open throttle, but the rest of the time, it ought to be close to right.

"When we fired the truck up for the first time, the guys working on it took it out and did burnouts for 2 hours and never did change the calibration. For all its life, it thought it really was a 1986 TPI Camaro. That's how the first fuel-injected big-block was born.

"Around that time, we were scrapping a Corvette and we brought a big-block in to see if it would fit in the en-

gine compartment. We took the small-block out and put the big-block in for about 15 minutes just to see if it would physically bolt in and clear the steering and what we call the 'wonderbar'—that bar that goes between the frame rails up around the water pump—and indeed it did.

"Well, the furor it created among the enthusiasts at the proving grounds here! For days, they kept coming over looking for the Corvette with the big-block in it. It was just an exercise in 'would it fit?' Having realized it would indeed fit, later on, I wanted to proceed with that as a second project.

"The Big Doggie got built because I bumped into Jim Minneker, the head of Corvette Powertrain. I showed him pictures of my truck and I said, 'We need to put one of these in a Corvette'—the first time I met the guy. And he said: 'You're right. Go for it.' I called the guys up that build the ma-

rine engines in GM Powertrain and talked with Ron Genaw and asked him about camshafts. He said he would send me a camshaft. Well, soon after that, an entire marine engine showed up—a camshaft wrapped in engine.

"Then we took an aftermarket tunnel ram manifold, added bosses for the fuel injectors, milled it 3/8in to make it lower, then lowered the plenum so it wasn't as tall as the one in the truck. Ultimately, we put a power bulge in the hood to clear the engine.

"My dyno was the Big Doggie, weighing 3,500 pounds and running 13-second ETs. With a 3.08 rear axle, I was guessing between 178mph and 185mph top speed. Big Doggie has long legs. The other interesting thing is with that 3.08 rear axle, in sixth gear, 2000rpm is 100mph. Interesting numbers. We ran it about two years before going public with it. The car now has aluminum heads and doesn't

With hood raised, enthusiasts admire the TPI 454 in the ZR2 at the 1990 Bloomington Gold event. Although never intended for production, the ZR2 has inspired Corvette owners with small-block V-8s to swap up and learn the true meaning of big-block power. Thomas Glatch

weigh more than a comparable ZR-1."

Without the tacit endorsement of Minneker, the ZR2 might never have been built. He had worked in the Pontiac Division with release responsibility as a powertrain supervisor on the Chevrolet Cavalier and Pontiac Sunbird four-cylinder engines, then as supervisor in the newly formed Chevrolet-Pontiac-Canada Division in 1985. In 1986, he was asked if he wanted to be chief engineer of Corvette Powertrain and he leapt at the opportunity. He explained his thinking behind doing a big-block Corvette:

"There were a couple of reasons for

Chevrolet kept the legendary LS6 and LS7 big-blocks in production until the advent of the new Mark series in 1991. This ad appeared in 1989 to announce the availability of the 350 H.O. and reminded bowtie fans that the LS6 was as close as the nearest parts counter. Reprint courtesy of GM Service Parts Operations

doing it. Around that time—1988—the older, current-generation cars of 1984 and 1985 were suffering in the used car marketplace. I thought that if there was a way to boost the resale value of these cars, it might be through a high-performance engine retrofit. If the tuners knew you could fit the big-block engine into the Corvette, that might cause buyers to go out and do that, and hence the value of those cars would go up.

"The other reason," Minneker added, "was I suspected that as we went into introduction with the LT5, the question for me was: 'Well, all the high technology is nice, but what about a big-block? What would that have done?' There was really no way to make an A-B comparison unless we actually had one put in a car."

Numerous magazines wrote enthusiastically about the ZR2; they all agreed the 454 Corvette, circa 1989, was a great car, but for a number of reasons, it would probably never see production, as some editors wished out loud in those articles. To begin with, it had performance that rivaled that of the LT5 engine in the ZR-1 Corvette; Chevrolet did not want a big-block Corvette competing against its performance flagship, the ZR-1. In addition, the 454's gas consumption would make it liable to the gas guzzler tax, which to Chevrolet is anathema. The ZR2 was really intended as an exercise in letting the hot rod community see that it was indeed possible to put a 454ci big-block V-8 in the Corvette.

Still, the ZR2 exercise produced positive fallout in that it drew attention to the 454ci big-block V-8 and verified advances in induction technology that would find their way into other applications in the nineties.

The New Mark-series 454ci V-8

The 454ci big-block V-8 had been in production for almost two decades when plans were formulated not only to upgrade and improve the Mk IV engine, but to replace the aging tooling at the Tonawanda Engine Plant. Fred Frincke was responsible for establishing the new design criteria for the new-generation 454.

"About three years before I retired from Chevrolet in May 1990 as design coordinator of advanced projects, I set up specifications for the Mk V to come out in 1991," Frincke said. "Prior to my leaving, most of my time was spent laying out specifications for the Mk V engine and making presentations.

"Also at that time, the tooling at the Tonawanda Engine Plant was pretty old and worn out, so Engineering and Manufacturing got together and said, 'We need a new engine for these reasons.' We successfully obtained enough money to retool the cylinder block and the crankshafts. We wanted to make a more reliable, more precise, and higher-quality engine at lower cost. We had to do a lot of things to the engine to accommodate Manufacturing.

"We went to one-size bearings and one-size pistons. Previously, we had an inability to make a bore precisely. For most of my career, the engine plant assembly line had shelves and shelves full of pistons sitting next to the production line so they could select the right size. They'd measure the bore, mark it, then select a piston off the shelf compatible with how that bore turned out."

Much more precise machining of the bores, permitting one-size pistons, and more precise machining of the crankshafts, allowing the use of one-size bearings, were just two criteria set down for the new engine.

Numerous refinements and improvements were made to the new Mark-series 454ci V-8 introduced in 1991, and the unit was improved further for 1992. The cylinder block received structural revisions to reduce bore distortion. Foundry procedures were improved to reduce casting variability of cylinder walls. The portion of the engine block that previously required a separate oil cooler adapter was redesigned, eliminating the need for the adapter; the new engine block now had integral oil cooler provisions. The oil filter could now be mounted the same as it had been in automotive applications.

A concerted effort was made to reduce or eliminate oil and coolant leaks. This included the adoption of a one-piece rear main seal; a one-piece molded oil pan gasket; a new diecast aluminum valve cover that had positive stop on the cylinder head surface and an O-ring seal on the threaded oil

fill cap; the elimination of the throttle body adapter, which was replaced with integral TBI mounting; and the elimination of the TBI coolant-heater hose.

The cylinder head featured a new net lash valvetrain. This eliminated the variation in valve lash with the old rocker arm mounting during assembly. In place of the rocker arm stud was a shouldered bolt with a positive stop.

Although none of these improvements were designed to increase the engine's performance, they did make for a much better big-block for truck users. For 1992, the L19 with a 7.9:1

compression ratio was rated at 230hp at 3600rpm and 385lb-ft of torque at a leisurely 1600rpm. Chevrolet decided to showcase these improvements in a new truck offering that brought back memories of big-block performance gone by.

The 454 SS Pickup

Chevrolet introduced the 454 SS pickup in 1990, installing the last run of the Mk IV 454ci V-8s. It was in 1991 that this performance sport truck came with the new Mark big-block. The 454ci V-8 had always been available in Chevrolet's line of full-size

The 454ci big-block V-8 has remained in production for more than 30 years. It has been a mainstay in Chevrolet trucks but is also used in motor homes and marine ap- *plications. The fuel delivery of this L19 is by means of a twin-bore throttle body injector. GM Powertrain*

trucks, but this truck was different in its concept and execution. And Chevrolet pitched to readers of the enthusiast magazines in an extensive ad campaign. It gave the 454 visibility it never had before.

The engine in the 454 SS pickup came with a higher-rated output than did the standard 454 available in other trucks. *Chevy Action* magazine tested a 1991 model in the fall of that year. The engine was rated at 255hp at 4000rpm and 405lb-ft of torque at 2400rpm. Despite its curb weight of 4,310 pounds, the standard 4.10 rear axle ratio—not available in Chevrolet's other trucks—helped push the 454 SS machine to 60mph in 7.7 seconds. The vehicle covered the quarter-mile in 15.7 seconds doing 85.9mph. The editors of *Chevy Action* wrote, "The 454 SS delivers levels of acceleration and cornering previously unheard of in a truck and wraps it all up with a big-block exhaust rumble that'll excite anyone who remembers the musclecar era."

The 454 HO

When GM Powertrain upgraded the assembly line at Tonawanda to build and assemble the new Mark series engine with its net lash valvetrain and numerous other refinements in the cylinder block and cylinder heads, production halted on the legendary LS6 and LS7 high-performance crate engines. This left an obvious void, and those at Chevrolet, GM Powertrain, and the Raceshop were all aware of it. Before the switch was made, concerns were raised about offering a replacement, but development on the substitute couldn't begin until the new Mark series engine was in production. Not until then would an engine exist on which development work could be based.

Chevrolet, and later GM Powertrain, has for years designed and offered big-block V-8s specifically for marine applications. Not being held to rigorous emissions regulations, the marine engines were developed with higher specific output than truck applications. It was on the marine big-block engine that the new high-performance aftermarket 454 would be based.

E. O. ("Eli") Whitney graduated from the GM Institute in 1972 with a bachelor of mechanical engineering degree. He worked as a production and quality control supervisor in the differential plant at Pontiac and as a process engineer in the crankshaft area of the 2.5-liter Iron Duke four-cylinder engine. In the late eighties, he became involved with the big-block in marine applications as part of Mark Engine Basic Design.

"There are two levels of the marine big-block," Whitney said. "The base marine engine, which is 310hp, and then the high-performance marine engine, which is in excess of 370hp. The 370hp 454 marine engine is originally derived from the LS6 454. We kept the compression down to a manageable 8.6:1 and used a hydraulic lifter cam instead of a solid lifter cam for reasons of maintenance. There are

For 1991, the new Mark series was introduced with numerous improvements. It was rated at 230hp at 3600rpm and 385lb-ft of torque at a leisurely 1600rpm. GM Powertrain

certain parts changed for specific marine use. We always use Inconel material exhaust valves and heavier inlet valves because of the heavy loads that are used in marine applications."

The task of adapting the 454 marine big-block for street use was given to Mark McPhail working out of Mc-Farland, Inc., in Torrance, California. McFarland acts essentially as the West Coast operations of the Raceshop, now known as GM Motorsports Technology Group, and is owned by Jim McFarland, who has long been affiliated with Chevrolet in various capacities. McPhail joined Chevrolet in 1985, after graduating from Michigan Technological University with a bachelor of science in mechanical engineering.

While a resident engineer at the Arlington, Texas, assembly plant, he spoke to engineers within the Raceshop and learned they were looking for a drag racing program manager. McPhail jumped at the chance. He became involved with a 502ci big-block engine project for an enthusiast magazine and was then asked if he wanted to move to California to work at Mc-Farland. McPhail's job there would be to coordinate high-performance Chevrolet vehicle and engine projects and promote them through the enthusiast magazines. He was involved with the development of the 454 High Output (HO) from the start.

"We couldn't make the LS6 and LS7 anymore because the new 454 has a net lash valvetrain and we couldn't incorporate the solid lifter cam profile," McPhail said. "We had to come up with an alternative. Also, the compression ratios were a little high on the LS6 and LS7 for street use.

"We took the 454 high-perfor-

The 454 SS pickup was introduced in 1990. It gave the big-block visibility on the street that had been absent since the early 1970s. You could order any color, as long as it was black.

mance marine engine assembly, advanced the cam 5 degrees, and put on the truck rocker arm covers. The engines were dynoed here at McFarland, Inc. We baselined the LS6 engine to see where we were. The 454 HO was down somewhat in horsepower, but it was our goal to have something compatible with premium unleaded pump-grade fuel. The intake manifold was the same part used on the LS6. We used a 750cfm Holley carb to run the tests."

The outputs developed by the old LS6 and the new 454 HO were very similar—within several horsepower

121

and pounds-feet of torque throughout the rpm range. The engines were run with 2in primary headers and 3.5in collectors mated to 2.5in exhaust pipes. The peak torque for the 454 HO occurred at approximately 3400rpm and was roughly 460lb-ft. At 5200rpm, the new big-block was putting out 425hp on the dyno.

Specifications for the engine include four-bolt main bearing caps; a marine hydraulic cam, part number 10185060; a single-roller timing chain; high-performance open-chamber rectangular port cylinder heads with 118cc combustion chambers using 2.19in-diameter intake valves and 1.88in-diameter exhaust valves; a forged 1053 steel crankshaft; and a 0.51in-lift hydraulic camshaft. The cast-aluminum high-rise intake manifold sports the snowflake foundry mark of Winters Foundry in Ohio, the same foundry that handled the aluminum castings on the L88 and ZL-1 engines. In the 454 HO, Chevrolet and GM Performance Parts have a worthy successor to their solid lifter Mk IV siblings.

The 502ci Big-block

To meet the needs of off-road and offshore users requiring the utmost in power, the 502ci big-block was developed.

"The 502 is the largest production displacement of the big-block in its history," Eli Whitney said. "It came about to meet the need of very large cruiser boats, as an alternative to diesels. Simultaneously, there was also a need for a higher-horsepower engine in speedboats. The 502 uses a large-bore siamesed block with a 454 crankshaft. To accommodate the large bore size with the 4in-stroke 454 crank, we ended up using the bow-tie block with siamesed bore. That was our starting point. We have a 4.4662in bore with a 4in stroke, which gives us our 502ci. We use an 8.75:1 compression ratio using JE forged aluminum pistons with a high-performance marine cam. It develops 380hp at 4600rpm.

"In the adaptation of that engine by the Raceshop for the performance parts catalog, that engine produces 430hp at 5200rpm. With open headers, it's in the 450hp range. We started this in the Mk IV series in the 1989–90 period. As we evolved into the new Mark series, we developed the marine engine. Then, for the Raceshop, Mark McPhail took the 502 short-block and put in his street cam," said Whitney.

The 502ci short-block partial assembly was conceived to allow professional racers the flexibility to choose their own cam grinds and cylinder heads. This made sense because a full 502ci engine assembly would just be disassembled by the racers to use the parts of their choice. They have the option of installing GM performance parts or high-performance parts made by other manufacturers. Besides the forged 1053 crankshaft, the short-block gets forged steel connecting rods with 7/16in-diameter bolts and with a Moraine rod and main bearings.

In tests at McFarland, the 502 was fitted with the marine hydraulic camshaft and various cylinder heads. Oval port and square port cylinder heads were bolted to the engine, and tests run with open and closed exhaust systems. The engine developed over 450hp and 530lb-ft of torque at their respective rpm peaks.

With these ongoing efforts by Chevrolet, GM Performance Parts, and GM Motorsports Technology Group, it's clear to Chevrolet fans that the big-block V-8 will be around for many years to come.

Automotive Big-Block V-8 Chronology

Year	Displacement (In)	Carburetor	Output (Hp)	Engine Code
1958	348	4bbl	250	576A
	348	3x2bbl	280	573A
	348	4bbl	300	576B
	348	3x2bbl	315	573B
1959	348	4bbl	250	576A
	348	3x2bbl	280	573A
	348	4bbl	305	576B
	348	4bbl	320	577
	348	3x2bbl	335	574
1960	348	4bbl	250	576A
	348	3x2bbl	280	573A
	348	4bbl	305	576B
	348	4bbl	320	577
	348	3x2bbl	335	574
1961	348	4bbl	250	576A
	348	3x2bbl	280	573A
	348	4bbl	305	576B
	348	4bbl	340	590
	348	3x2bbl	350	573B
	409	4bbl	360	580
1962	409	4bbl	380	580
	409	2x4bbl	409	587
1963	409	4bbl	340	L33
	409	4bbl	400	L31
	409	2x4bbl	425	L80
	427	2x4bbl	425	Z11
1964	409	4bbl	340	L33
	409	4bbl	400	L31
	409	4bbl	425	L80

Year	Displacement (In)	Carburetor	Output (Hp)	Engine Code
1965	396	4bbl	325	L35
	396	4bbl	375	L37
	396	4bbl	425	L78
	409	4bbl	340	L33
	409	4bbl	400	L31
1966	396	4bbl	325	L35
	396	4bbl	360	L34
	396	4bbl	375	L78
	427	4bbl	390	L36
	427	4bbl	425	L72
1967	396	4bbl	325	L35
	396	4bbl	350	L34
	396	4bbl	375	L78
	427	4bbl	385	L36
	427	4bbl	390	L36
	427	3x2bbl	400	L68
	427	3x2bbl	435	L71
	427	4bbl	430	L88
1968	396	4bbl	325	L35
	396	4bbl	350	L34
	396	4bbl	375	L78
	427	4bbl	385	L36
	427	4bbl	390	L36
	427	3x2bbl	400	L68
	427	4bbl	425	L72
	427	4bbl	430	L88
	427	3x2bbl	435	L71
1969	396	2bbl	265	L66
	396	4bbl	325	L35
	396	4bbl	350	L34
	396	4bbl	375	L78
	427	4bbl	335	LS1
	427	4bbl	390	L36
	427	3x2bbl	400	L68
	427	4bbl	425	L72
	427	4bbl	430	L88
	427	4bbl	430	ZL-1
	427	3x2bbl	435	L71
1970	402	4bbl	330	LS3
	402	4bbl	350	L34
	402	4bbl	375	L78
	454	4bbl	345	LS4
	454	4bbl	360	LS5
	454	4bbl	390	LS5
	454	4bbl	450	LS6
	454	4bbl	460	LS7
1971	402	4bbl	300	LS3
	454	4bbl	365	LS5
	454	4bbl	425	LS6
1972	402	4bbl	210	LS3
	402	4bbl	240	LS3
	454	4bbl	230	LS5
	454	4bbl	270	LS5

Year	Displacement (In)	Carburetor	Output (Hp)	Engine Code
1973	454	4bbl	215	LS4
	454	4bbl	245	LS4
	454	4bbl	275	LS4
1974	454	4bbl	235	LS4
	454	4bbl	270	LS4
1975	454	4bbl	235	LS4
1976	454	4bbl	225	LS4

Sources: *Chevrolet Division Engine Application Chart, 1958–1972*. This Chevrolet Engineering document records both small-block and big-block V-8s, including vehicle applications, outputs, carburetion setups, and engine codes.
Chevrolet Advertised Engine Ratings, 1960–1966. These documents list the horsepower, torque, and compressions ratios for both small-block and big-block V-8s used in passenger cars and Corvettes. They are signed by Maurice S. Rosenberger.

Michael Bruce, *Corvette Black Book, 1953–1992* (Michael Bruce Associates, November 1991).

Pat Chappell, *Standard Catalog of Chevrolet, 1912–1990* (Krause Publications, 1990).

Big-Block V-8 Engine Specifications

Big-Block V-8 Engine Specifications

Engine	348	409	427 (W)	MK IIS	396	402
Bore (in)	4.125	4.31	4.31	4.31	4.094	4.125
Stroke (in)	3.25	3.5	3.65	3.65	3.76	3.76
Crankshaft	Forged steel	Forged steel	Forged steel	Forged steel	Forged steel	Cast iron
Main bearing diameter (in)	2.5	2.5	2.5	2.5	2.748	2.748
Connecting rod bearing diameter (in)	2.2	2.2	2.2	2.2	2.2	2.2
Connecting rod bolt diameter (in)	$3/8$	$3/8$	$3/8$	$3/8$	$3/8$	$3/8$
Connecting rod length (in)	6.135	6.135	6.01	6.01	6.135	6.135
Inlet valve diameter (in)	1.94	2.06	2.19	2.19	2.065	2.065
Exhaust valve diameter (in)	1.66	1.72	1.72	1.72	1.72	1.72
Block deck height (in)	9.8	9.8	9.8	9.8	9.8	9.8
Bearing cap bolts	2	2	2	2	2 or 4	2 or 4

Engine	427	454	482	502	366 (Truck)	427 (Truck)
Bore (in)	4.251	4.251	4.251	4.466	3.938	4.251
Stroke (in)	3.76	4	4.25	4	3.76	3.76
Crankshaft	Forged steel	Cast iron	Forged steel	Forged steel	Forged steel	Forged steel
Main bearing diameter (in)	2.748	2.748	2.748	2.748	2.748	2.748

Engine	427	454	482	502	366 (Truck)	427 (Truck)
Connecting rod bearing diameter (in)	2.2	2.2	2.2	2.2	2.2	2.2
Connecting rod length (in)	6.135	6.135	6.405	6.135	6.135	6.135
Connecting rod bolt diameter (in)	$^3/_8$	$^3/_8$	$^7/_{16}$	$^7/_{16}$	$^3/_8$	$^3/_8$
Inlet valve diameter (in)	2.065	2.065	2.19	2.19	1.84	1.84
Exhaust valve diameter (in)	1.72	1.72	1.72	1.72	1.66	1.66
Block deck height (in)	9.8	9.8	10.2	9.8	10.2	10.2
Bearing cap bolts	2 or 4	2 or 4	4	4	4	4

Notes:

1. The prefix of the suffix code on the engine block will be *T* for "Tonawanda." The date code is the next four numbers: the first two are the month, and the last two are the day the engine was built. For example, T0321 means "Built at Tonawanda on March 21." Regarding the last letters in the suffix code, W-series block engines can have single-letter codes and all Mark engines will have two- or three-letter codes. Some Mk IV engines built in 1965 and 1966 will have the letter *H* or *R* on the end of their two-letter suffix; this stands for a Holley or Rochester carburetor. Some 1969 396ci V-8 suffix codes can begin with a *C* or a *T*; this signifies a 402ci displacement. Beginning with the 1970 model year, Mark engines began with a *C* or a *T*; the *C* stood for "passenger car," and the *T* stood for "truck."

2. All engines built before 1967 had forged steel crankshafts. In 1967, the change was made to nodular cast-iron crankshafts in low-performance engines. Generally speaking, all two-bolt engines built in 1968 and later had cast crankshafts; all four-bolt engines had forged crankshafts.

3. Solid lifter engines in the Mk IV series had $^7/_{16}$in premium rod bolts and rods.

4. Some high-performance 348s built after mid-1959 had 2.065in-diameter intake valves. High-performance 409s with 690 or 583 head castings had 2.19in-diameter intake valves. The 409ci truck engines had 1.94in-diameter intake valves. Mk IV high-performance engines—those with solid lifters and rectangular port heads—had 2.19in-diameter intake valves.

5. L88s for 1967 and 1968 had 1.84in-diameter exhaust valves, which were increased to 1.88in in diameter for 1969. ZL-1s, LS6s, and LS7s had 1.88in-diameter exhaust valves.

6. High-performance Mk IV engines with solid lifter camshafts had four-bolt main bearing caps, as did all 366ci and 427ci tall-deck truck engines and all big-block engines built after 1987.

Source: Art Casper, Tonawanda Engine Plant.

Index